MANIPULATION PSYCHOLOGY

BEGINNERS GUIDE TO MASTERING THE BEST NLP AND PSYCHOLOGY TECHNIQUES, TO IMPROVE EMPATHY AND THE ART OF SEDUCTION AND ATTRACTION.

John Austin

Copyright © 2020 by John Austin. All Rights Reserved.

No part of this book may be reproduced, stored in retrieval systems,or transmitted by any means, electronic, mechanical,photocopying, recorded or otherwise withoutwritten permission from the author.

Published by Mybook Self-Publishing Ltd

Table of Contents

Introduction

Manipulation is also referred to as "psychological manipulation." Psychologists think of psychological manipulation as "undue influence on a person or a group of people." That undue influence can be realized through "mental distortion" or through "emotional exploitation." When mental distortion is engaged, we call that mind manipulation. When emotional exploitation is engaged, we call it emotional manipulation.

Mind manipulation techniques, as we have said, are those that distort the way a person thinks. These techniques work by either reducing a person's ability to think in a logical or critical way, or by changing the beliefs, values, attitudes, and assumptions that a person makes when he perceives certain things.

We fall for mind manipulation techniques because our belief systems are altered, and as a result, we truly believe the assertions that the manipulator is making at the moment.

Emotional manipulation techniques, on the other hand, play with the way a person feels towards either the manipulator or other people that the manipulator is leveraging. We fall for emotional manipulation techniques either because we want to please other people, or because we want to prove something to them.

Mind manipulation techniques are methods of influence that disrupt people to their very cores. They alter the very things that a person uses to define himself; they can change his identity.

When mind manipulation techniques are effectively deployed, they can temporarily give a person a new outlook (this true in cases of milder forms of mind manipulation such as mind games) or they can completely overhaul a person's very identity and replace it with a new "pseudo-personality" (this is true in cases where extreme forms of mind manipulation, such as brainwashing are used).

Emotional manipulation techniques, on the other hand, are methods of influence which change a person's "emotional priorities." They alter the way the subject feels towards a specific person, relative to the way he or she feels about himself or herself, or other people.

When a person uses emotional manipulation against you, you feel a sense of obligation to do what they want because you are emotionally invested in their wellbeing, or because you are afraid of certain emotional consequences that you'll suffer if you don't do what they want.

In both mind manipulation and emotional manipulation, the manipulator takes advantage of the trust that's is bestowed on him or her by the victim.

In relationship dynamics, that trust can take the form of affection. You are more susceptible to manipulation from people who you hold in high esteem: it could be a man or woman you are sexually attracted to; it could be a boss who you have a professional obligation to respect; it could be a charismatic leader whose ideas you like.

For any kind of manipulation to work, there has to be some common ground between the victim and the manipulator. So, in a way, manipulation can be seen as a violation of trust.

Mind and emotional manipulation also take advantage of a person's good-natured. "Good people" are more susceptible to manipulation than "bad people." If you are a person of goodwill, a fair-minded person, you are more likely to trust people implicitly, to give them the benefit of the doubt, and to indulge them even when they make you uncomfortable. That's because your brain operates under the premise that people are generally good; even if you suspect that a person has an ulterior motive, you'll still go out of your way to treat them with decency and to be considerate towards them.

Everyone is susceptible to mind and emotional manipulation. It's easy for you to assume that you are too smart to be manipulated, or that you are too emotionally stable for someone to play with your emotions, but that's a myth that we should dispel from the very beginning of this book. No one is too smart to be manipulated. As long as you have thoughts and feelings, someone can manipulate them.

If you are very smart and unfailingly logical, someone can use a well thought out logical argument to convince you to behave in a certain way. If you feel strongly for the people in your life, those people (or other third parties) can use those feeling to control your behavior.

The worst thing you can do is assume that only foolish or careless people get manipulated. You too can be victimized by a manipulative person, through no fault of your own. To protect or defend yourself against manipulation, the first thing you have to do is acknowledge the fact that you are vulnerable to it.

Most manipulation techniques out there utilize both mental and emotional aspects, so it can be difficult to distinctly categorize certain techniques as either mind manipulation techniques or emotional manipulation techniques. Sometimes, the way we think and the way we feel can be closely intertwined in such a way that it becomes impossible to unlink them.

One such technique is the manipulation of facts. When someone manipulates facts, they are messing with both the way you think and the way you feel. So, manipulation of facts can be seen as both a mind and an emotional technique.

That explains why many popular psychologists don't bother making the distinction between the two. Most of them lump all manipulation techniques together because they believe that at the end of the day, manipulation is manipulation; it doesn't matter if it's mental or emotional.

I don't buy into that argument. I believe that the distinction is important because it helps you to understand the working mechanism of each manipulation technique, and the better you understand all techniques, the more likely you are to triumph over the machinations of the manipulative people in your life.

Deception Through Gas Lighting

It is almost impossible to break someone's walls when he is certain about his own convictions. You may encounter impossible people that would willingly bring you to court or challenge you to an endless debate just to prove that he is right. When things come to this point, there is a technique used by many manipulators when they feel that they are in a bad position when it comes to convincing their targets. This technique is called gas lighting.

The Power of Self-Doubt

Gas lighting as a term is believed to have originated from a stage play wherein a character makes his wife believe that she is going insane by subtly changing her environment, which would involve slowly making the flame on her gas lamp go dim. Now, the term is used to describe techniques devised by manipulators to establish doubt in their target's minds in order for them to step in and gain control of the situation.

The technique is sophisticated and it takes a while before it may work when you do not know the target that well. However, if you are very good at playing poker, you may feel that this is part of any game that requires some mental trickery.

The main element of this mind trick is the mentalist's ability to establish doubt in the mind of his target. However, it is more than the doubt that you feel when you think that you are being lied to. When you perform this technique, you are establishing to your target that he may not be fit to make a decision, hence, the establishment of self-doubt.

When a person doubts himself, the punishment that he creates against himself goes a long way. The mere fact that he cannot trust his own judgment produces great anxiety. When one is not sure about the consequences of his actions, he is led to do one thing, which is to search for another solution. The manipulator easily comes in and tells his target what to do.

How to Do Gas Lighting

There are several factors that you need to consider when you do gas lighting. The key to perform it successfully is to establish the following:

A series of truths and vague untruths

When you want to change the environment of the target and make him believe that the conditions have already changed, then you need to create a list of true things. For example, you know that you are inside your room when you see your favorite pillow on your bed, or when you see your personal lampshade. However, you feel that you are not there when you do not see them. If these things are transferred into another room with the same layout, you can easily be misled into thinking that that different room is yours. How would you feel when you are told that you entered the wrong room? You become anxious at the thought of it. The next time you enter your true room, you would feel paranoid. You feel that someone might be playing tricks on you again.

The establishment of yourself as an authority

To assume the role of the manipulator, you need to make sure that your target believes you when he is not sure of his own judgment. Following the above example, when you change the layout of your target's bedroom and he is not sure whether he is entering the right room or not, you should assume authority that you know that it is his. Tell him another series of truths, for example that he is in the right room, or that someone just changed the bed sheets. Tell him where his pillow is. Because of his anxiety, he is likely to believe you when you give the proof that you actually know what is going on.

The direction you need the target to follow

Think of the situation wherein your target is unsure of whether he is in his own room or not as a proof that he needs to doubt himself and seek your advice whenever he enters his house. Establishing a similar scenario would allow you to have a playing card in your hand whenever you need to drive your target in a specific direction. You can always say that previously he was not sure about where he was, and that is also the situation now.

Since you have established yourself as the person who knows the truth, he would be bound to ask for your help. At this point, you can tell him what you want him to believe, and following that, what he should do next.

The Manipulator as the Shedder of Light

Gas lighting as a deception technique will only work if you are able to make it a point that your target will believe that you are the only one who can tell him what to do and that you are the only one who can tell what is true or not. In a lot of situations, being the most credible person in the room is difficult to achieve. For that reason, it is very important that you plant the seeds of your credibility.

It also means that performing this trick can be very difficult or time-consuming, since it may require you to subtly imply to the target that he is wrong and you are always right. Doing so would require you to make changes to his environment little by little, and then point them out whenever you do so. It is like teaching your target how to learn a different language or how to use a code. In a way, it may require you to actually alter what he knows about himself and how he should react to things that he normally encounters.

While this technique may take a long while to be perfected, it provides a strong hold on your target's belief, and like any great deception, the changes that he went through and how you staged all of them would be very hard for him to detect.

You are the only one who really knows what's going on, and even bystanders cannot see all the things that you have done in order to perform the trick. Since you are the only one who knows all the elements in his environment that you managed to change little by little, it becomes easy for your target to just surrender to everything that you are saying and uphold them as the truth.

When you think about it, this same technique is used by most mentalists and street magicians who have already set up the stage to any unsuspecting target. While their targets think that they see an ordinary box or ordinary deck of cards that might have a bit of surprise, they do not really look at where the deception is happening. By being able to make targets focus on another thing that is suspicious, the "magic" is already happening somewhere else that is undetectable. The magician makes a number of true statements, and then when the trick is performed, the target will always question what he just saw. Because he cannot tell how the trick was performed and when exactly the deception occurred, he just surrenders to the thought that it is, in fact, magic.

However, when you perform gas lighting over an extended amount of time, you risk the danger of exposing where the trick is happening, but when you get past that risk and the traps go unnoticed, you can perform this technique again and again to the unsuspecting target. It is like stealing credit card information and making little purchases that are hard to notice. When the bill arrives and the credit card owner wonders why he needs to pay more than he usually does, he is bound to look on the statement for large purchases, which of course, he made himself. Should he suspect that something is wrong and he asks the manipulator, he would still be made to look for the larger charges and be convinced that it is his own fault that the bill is more than usual. Why gas lighting always works is because you tell the truth, but not its entirety. The main part of the deceit is to hide the little, often harmless lies, that when put together, create an elaborate deception that is enough to make the target confuse reality with fabrication.

Practical Uses of Gas Lighting

This technique has a lot of practical forms, but it is particularly useful when you are defending yourself from any accusation. For example, if someone accuses you of lying, you can make use of gas lighting to make that statement backfire on your accuser by proving that there have been circumstances wherein he was not sure whether he knew the truth or not, and you are the one who can tell him. By saying so, you make it seem to him that it is unreasonable for him to make his claim when he was not even sure what the truth was.

You will probably encounter this technique in courtrooms, where lawyers throw in this trick in order to discredit a witness. By saying that the witness has bouts of paranoia or has a previous history where he cannot even tell whether he is in good mental health, his credibility is shattered. The lawyer that is interrogating him easily manipulates him into retracting what he just said, or agreeing to another truth. Even if the witness refuses to agree to what the lawyer is trying to establish, there is still leverage for the interrogating side, and that damages the reputation of the witness.

Even if you are not practicing law, you can take advantage of the positive results that this brings you when you are in sales or in customer service. There are a lot of situations where customers complain about products, without having first read the manual or turning the item on. When you state the fact that there are many situations where customers do not use the product for its intended purpose, or that many have failed to follow simple instructions which would solve more than 90% of the problem, they will begin to doubt themselves and the real reason why they are making a complaint in the first place. What they are likely to do is to end the call and think where they could possibly have gone wrong. Not only would that save you time trying to repeat instructions that they could find by themselves, you possibly do them a service by making them find solutions instead of you.

Some Notes to Keep in Mind

You need to take a lot of caution when you use gas lighting – it can backfire on you if you try to do the trick too quickly. The reason is that anyone can discover major environmental changes and detect the potential of deception. Once they put the doubt on you, and not on themselves, it would be very hard to perform any manipulative or deceptive techniques on your target. Should that happen, you would need to make sure that you prove your trustworthiness by telling them a number of true reasons why you should be trusted and suggest he question himself for feeling it necessary to doubt you. When you are able to pull that off, you successfully planted self-doubt, which is key to this technique. However, you need to watch your step – it does not mean that when the target doubts himself, he has no reason to doubt you, too.

Chapter 1 Neuro-Linguistic Programming (NLP)?

NLP sounds confusing, but the title is quite misleading. Anyone can learn NLP, which means it can be used for good and bad. We should point out here and now that at its very core, NLP is supposed to be used as self-development and improvement tool, it is not supposed to be used as a way to control others. Unfortunately, some unscrupulous types have learned how to use this very technique for bad rather than good.

First things first, let's explain what NLP actually is.

NLP was founded back in the 1970s by Richard Bandler and John Grinder. This is a way of communicating with the mind. The idea behind NLP is that there is a direct link between language and behavior, with the brain's neurological processes, e.g. thoughts and suggestion.

NLP can be used for good reasons, e.g. it has been used to help with depression, learning disorders, phobias, and damaging habits. This is all done by controlling the mind, i.e. telling it what you want it to do and persuading it, via your words, to do that exact thing.

NLP works because it taps into patterns. If you think about your general life, you probably have a pattern for everything, e.g. how you get up in the mornings, how you go to bed, how you eat, how you prepare to go out in the evenings. We are creatures of habit. These habits are formed because there is a chemical reaction between the thoughts that our mind conjure up and the things we do. This means that every action in that pattern is performed because of a thought, which can either be conscious or it can be unconscious, i.e. not something you're aware of. NLP, therefore, uses patterns and words to train the brain to think or do a certain thing.

NLP can help change the way you see the world, and that sentence in itself tells you why manipulators effectively use this technique to trap someone in a particular pattern of thinking. Remember, our feelings and our thoughts are what create our own version of reality, and when these are altered, our version of reality is also altered.

Two positive and useful NLP exercises include:

Disassociation

This particular Technique is ideal for helping to get rid of a particular emotion or feeling that you find troubling.

Disassociation means identifying the thing you want to get rid of, i.e. shyness, and then identifying the emotion which goes along with it, so nervousness perhaps in this case. You would then close your eyes and imagine yourself floating above your body, and seeing the situation from the outside, looking in. You will notice that you feel different about it instantly because it's not happening to you at that moment. Using this technique when situations peak is a great way to avoid negative emotions from taking hold.

Reframing

Reframing means identifying a negative that you constantly tell yourself and giving it an alternative explanation, i.e. a positive slant. For instance, maybe you lose your job. Firstly that is terrible and you're going to feel bad for a while, but you can reframe your emotions by coming up with something positive and putting it on repeat. In this situation, you might think about the fact you can retrain and finally do the one thing you've always wanted to do. This allows you to see negative experiences as less life-changing and terrible, and simply as ways to change direction and perhaps learn.

There are countless other NLP exercises and it's really something that you need to dedicate time to in order to learn how it can be useful to you. What we need to explore however is how the language of your brain and influencing it can be used against you, i.e. in the hands of a manipulator.

You might be looking at those two exercises and wonder how a manipulator could use them for negative, but these are simple explanations of what this technique is about. By reading about these techniques you can understand that you're influencing your thoughts by telling your brain what you want it to think and therefore believe. We act on our thoughts, so your actions will mirror what you're thinking.

When a manipulator constantly tells you something, i.e. "you're useless", the more you hear it, the more you start to believe it. In the end, your actions start to mirror your thoughts. So, you'll start doing less, trying less, not reaching out for new opportunities, and in the end, your manipulator has won, because you're dumbed down, firmly in their clutches.

The human brain also learns by repetition. Think back to when you were a child and you were learning the alphabet. Can you remember the alphabet song? Of course you can, you all sang it several times during a school day! The reason you can still remember it is because of that repetitive action that your school teacher imparted on you. In some ways, that's NLP. We learn via NLP techniques. So, when you hear negative phrases about yourself from someone you trust and care about, your brain believes them.

So, to sum up, NLP is a way of communicating with the mind and changing the thoughts that it creates, therefore changing actions at the same time. It's supposed to be a positive technique to help people get over difficult situations and negative emotions, but in the wrong hands, it can be used with very damaging consequences.

Chapter 2 Learning how to recognize and acknowledge the problem

The first step in this process is learning how to recognize and acknowledge the problem. If you are a victim of manipulation, this step is one of the hardest ones there is. Your partner may try to manipulate you into believing that there is not, in fact, any problem at all.

But armed with the information in this chapter, you will be better able to see the situation more clearly and understand that he or she is trying to manipulate you. To begin, answer the questions in the quiz below and then read about your results.

Answer as honestly as possible. This quiz is not meant to give you a 100% definitive answer about whether or not you are in a manipulative relationship. Instead, this is just to help you get oriented and ready to think carefully and examine your relationship more deeply. You can get a general sense of where you are at and learn what kind of questions you need to be asking yourself as you work your way through this process.

The Manipulative Relationship Quiz

1. Does your partner make negative or hurtful comments about you to friends or other people?

a) Never (1 point)

b) Rarely (2 points)

c) Sometimes (3 points)

d) Often (4 points)

2. Does your partner insult or criticize you or put you down?

a) Never (1 point)

b) Rarely (2 points)

c) Sometimes (3 points)

d) Often (4 points)

3. When your partner wants to do something but you do not want to do it, you:

a) Voice your opinion and suggest an alternative (1 point)

b) Voice your opinion but remain open to compromise (2 points)

c) Try to convince him or her not to do it without actually coming out and saying that you do not want to (3 points)

d) Keep your opinion to yourself and just do it anyway. You would rather avoid a fight. (4 points)

4. When you and your partner fight, how does it usually look?

a) You both take the time to express your own emotions as well as listen to the other. Sometimes you lose your temper but you always try to remain calm and supportive (1 point)

b) We each express our own emotions but sometimes have trouble listening to each other when it is really emotional. But no matter what, we are honest with each other. (2 points)

c) I have difficulty expressing emotions and I often get the feeling he or she also isn't saying the full truth. (3 points)

d) I usually avoid fights and have difficulty expressing my emotions. My partner typically gets very angry very quickly. (4 points)

5. When you and your partner fight, how does it end?

a) You work out some solution that satisfies both of you as much as possible. No matter what, you make sure it is completely resolved (1 point).

b) You work out a compromise that you can both agree to. Sometimes there is still some left over disappointment but for the most part, you reach an understanding. (2 points)

c) You both try to work out a compromise but often, you just end up ignoring the problem until it comes up again. (3 points)

d) Your fights usually end with you giving in and your partner getting his or her way. You just want to get it over with as soon as possible. (4 points)

6) If your partner says or does something that upsets you, you:

a) Tell him or her what has upset you and why in a calm way and ask him or her to make an effort to stop the behavior. He or she makes an honest effort to respect your wishes. (1 point)

b) Tell him or her what has upset you and why as calmly and possible and tell him or her to stop. But he or she does not always stop. (2 points)

c) Try to explain what is bothering you but sometimes he or she is difficult and doesn't listen. (3 points)

d) Keep your feelings to yourself and hope that he or she notices that it is bothering you without you having to say something. (4 points)

7. When you point out a problem in the relationship to your partner, he or she:

a) Listens, tries to understand, and then works with you to find a solution (1 point)

b) Listens, tries to understand, but you don't always see eye to eye about the issue. (2 points)

c) He or she becomes immediately upset and tries to deny that the problem exists. (3 points)

d) You would not try to point out a problem to your partner. He or she would become too upset. His or her reaction would be worse than just dealing with the problem on your own. (4 points)

8. Do you suspect your partner is cheating on you?

a) Never (1 point)

b) You have suspected it once or twice but it turned out to be nothing in the end. (2 points)

c) You have suspected quite a few times but aren't sure whether it's just your own insecurity or not. (3 points)

d) You have suspected it often (or you have proof that he or she has) but you are afraid to confront your partner about it. (4 points)

9. Have you ever done something that you otherwise would not do just to make your partner happy?

a) Never (1 point)

b) Rarely (2 points)

c) Sometimes (3 points)

d) Often (4 points)

10. Have you ever had sex with your partner (or performed some sexual act) even though you did not want to just to make him or her happy or avoid a fight?

a) Never (1 point)

b) Rarely (2 points)

c) Sometimes (3 points)

d) Often (4 points)

11. Does your partner threaten to leave you if he or she does not get his or her way?

a) Never (1 point)

b) Rarely (2 points)

c) Sometimes (3 points)

d) Often (4 points)

12. Does your partner bring up the past in order to make you feel guilty or bad about yourself?

a) Never (1 point)

b) Rarely (2 points)

c) Sometimes (3 points)

d) Often (4 points)

13. How often do you feel that your partner is hiding something from you (whether it is hiding something he or she has done, hiding his or her true emotions, or anything else)?

a) Never. You are always honest with each other and listen to each other without judgment (1 point)

b) Rarely. There have been a couple times that he or she was not sure how you would react to something but for the most part, you make sure you can be honest with each other without being afraid of the reaction (2 points)

c) Sometimes. There are certain topics or subjects you know not to try and bring up around your partner (3 points)

d) Often. Most of the time, you feel as if you have no idea what is really going on in your partner's head or how he or she will react to something. (4 points)

14. Between the two of you, which one tends to apologize more often?

a) It is basically equal. You both are willing to apologize when you see that you are at fault. (1 point)

b) It is basically equal but you occasionally get the feeling you are more willing to apologize than your partner is (2 points)

c) You apologize more often than your partner. He or she has difficulty acknowledging when he or she is at fault. (3 points)

d) It seems you are the only one who apologizes. Your partner never feels at fault for anything but demands that you apologize. If he or she does apologize, it never sounds genuine. (4 points)

15. How does your partner get along with your friends and family?

a) They get along with each other well. Some get along with him or her better than others but they are all on pleasant terms. (1 point)

b) They mostly get along with each other. Sometimes there is a little tension but 90% of the time, they are on pleasant terms (2 points)

c) My partner has difficulties getting along with my friends and family. They don't like him or her very much but they try to be nice. (3 points)

d) My partner does not get along with them at all. Most of the time he or she refuses to see them. You have started seeing your friends and family less as a result. (4 points)

16. Does your partner often encourage you to follow your dreams and do what makes you happy

a) Always (1 point)

b) Most of the time. (2 points)

c) Rarely. He or she expresses doubt that your dreams are realistic or worth following. (3 points)

d) Never. He or she makes you feel as if you could not accomplish them or tells you that what you want is stupid or not worth doing. He or she acts as if his or her own dreams and happiness are the most important. (4 points)

Quiz Results

Now that you have answered all the questions, go back and add up all your points to find out which result you got:

- 16 – 24 points: You are in a very healthy relationship. You both put in the necessary effort to make sure that your relationship is a source of happiness and security. You respect each other and love each other. Most importantly, you always make sure to show that to each other. When you do have problems (as every relationship always does), you always manage to find a solution that you can both live with. Keep up the good work. This one is a keeper!

- 25 – 38 points: You are in a healthy relationship. Both of you try to make the effort to keep the relationship strong. You love and respect each other. Most importantly, you genuinely care about how the other person feels. Sometimes you have some difficulties communicating or you forget to show how much you love and respect the person.

But these are small mistakes. Mistakes happen, you are both human. Just make a little extra effort to be completely honest with each other and find ways to show your love and respect for each other. Whatever problems you encounter along the way, this is a relationship worth saving.

- 39 – 51 points: You are in a borderline toxic relationship: Honesty does not come easily to either of you and expressing yourselves is a difficult task. You probably feel as if there is a divide between you and you aren't really sure how to get across it and reach a place of honesty and understanding.

Your partner (and perhaps you as well) have difficulty confronting problems especially when he or she is at fault. He or she will likely exhibit some of the signs of manipulative behavior that you will read about below. While your relationship is currently toxic and in a tough spot, there is still a chance that it has become so severe as to be irresolvable.

If you can re-establish honest communication and your partner is willing to meet you half way to work on this, the relationship could be made healthy and happy.

- 52 - 64 points: You are in a manipulative relationship: If you scored in this range, there is a very strong possibility that your partner is highly manipulative and that you are suffering in an extremely toxic relationship. Manipulative partners can cause a lot of emotional damage (and sometimes even physical).

If your relationship doesn't provide you with a source of happiness and security, then you need to take a step back and seriously consider your future. Read about the specific signs of manipulative behavior below. It is likely that many of them will sound familiar to you. Don't worry, though, there is always a way out and always way to turn your life around and find real love and happiness in the future.

As you may have noticed, many of the questions in the quiz dealt with how you and your partner deal with problems and fights. One of the main tests of a healthy relationship is how well you and your partner handle relationship issues. There is no such thing as a relationship without problems so fighting is not necessarily a bad thing.

The important thing is that even while fighting, you and your partner maintain respect and love for each other. This means that in any fight, your partner shows equal concern for his or her own emotions and yours (and you do the same for him or her).

Signs Your Partner is Manipulative

There are quite a few red flags that you can look for to determine whether or not you are in an abusive relationship. Some of them are more difficult to notice than others. And if you are the one being manipulated, it becomes especially difficult. But make the effort to look at your relationship objectively, from the outside and see if you can recognize any of these red flags in your partner's behavior:

- Negative or insulting: if your partner puts you down or belittles your accomplishments, this is a huge sign that he or she is manipulative. Insulting you or frequently being negative and rude toward you is a way of lowering your self-esteem so that you don't feel as if you deserve to be treated any better.

- Making threats: if your partner makes threats in order to get you to do something, he or she is definitely manipulating you. Threats can be anything from threatening to abandon you, threatening to hurt you, or threatening to cheat on you. Most likely, your partner will find what you fear the most and threaten you with it. Using someone's fear or guilt to get what you want is no way to treat a person that you love. There is no excuse for this kind of behavior in your relationship. None.

- Blaming and Accusing: in every relationship, there are some problems where it really is one person at fault. However, in most cases, when a problem arises, both people have helped cause it in some way. It takes two to tango. So if your partner is always blaming you or accusing you for every problem, he or she is trying to manipulate you into thinking the unhealthy relationship is entirely your fault. You should not allow yourself to carry the full burden of the blame. Your partner should acknowledge his or her part in causing the problems that the two of you have.

- Acting possessive or controlling: this is a very clear sign of manipulation. If your partner demands to know where you are and what you are doing every minute of the day, he or she is definitely trying to control you. If he or she tells you who you can and cannot see, this is manipulation.

In a healthy relationship, both partners trust each other and know that even if they are not with each other 24/7, they can still trust that the other is being faithful. This sort of trust is absolutely essential. Possessive and controlling behavior are not a healthy alternative to genuine trust.

- Showing a lack of respect: if your partner acts as if he or she does not care about how you feel or whether or not you are happy, it is likely because he or she really does not care. Yes, sometimes people forget to show how much they care. But if you find yourself constantly giving in to his or her wants and desires without ever having your own needs met, it is because your partner only cares about his or her own needs.

Relationships should be give and take. There should be a balance so that both of you are having your needs met rather than just you sacrificing everything for your partner.

Signs You Are Being Manipulated

After taking a hard look at your partner's behavior, it is time to turn around and take the same hard look at yourself. Do you show the signs of someone who is being manipulated? Read through these signs and see if you can relate to any of them:

- Low self-esteem: if you have always had low self-esteem, you are, unfortunately, more likely to fall for manipulative personalities. If you have only recently developed low self-esteem, it is likely the result of your partner's manipulative behavior. In either situation, your low self-esteem will continue to persist for as long as you allow yourself to be manipulated.

- Feelings of guilt: if you often feel guilty and find yourself often feeling ashamed about things that have happened long ago, this is a sign that you are being manipulated. Manipulative people thrive on your guilt. This is because the more strongly you feel guilt, the more easily you accept the blame for anything that goes wrong in the relationship. You begin to think that you must be a terrible person who is at fault for all of these issues. This frees your partner from having to accept any of the responsibility.

- Feelings of shame: if your partner is manipulative, he or she will likely try to make you feel as ashamed as possible. If you often feel ashamed of yourself (or ashamed of your partner), this is a sign that you are in a manipulative relationship. Healthy relationships are free of shame. Your partner should not judge you or put you down. Any criticism he or she may have will be given in a loving and constructive way that brings you up rather than puts you down.

- Depression: depression is a very common symptom of manipulative relationships. The longer the relationship persists, the more and more unhappy you will become. Eventually, you will start to feel completely hopeless and stop feeling any sort of happiness whatsoever.

Even the things that you once loved to do will seem pointless. This is a dangerous road to go down so if you have noticed yourself getting more and more depressed, you need to get out of the relationship immediately.

- Anxiety: if you feel heightened anxiety around your partner, you are probably being manipulated. Anxiety that he or she may react badly to something or feeling uncertain of how he or she will behave are signs of manipulation. In healthy relationships, you don't have to worry about these things. You can trust your partner enough to know that even if he or she is in a bad mood, they will not completely lash out at you or blame you for their problems.

A manipulative person, on the other hand, has very little control over his or her emotions. He or she can become angry or upset at the slightest trigger and then will promptly blame you for the outburst. Living with this kind of anxiety is something that you should not have to deal with in a relationship.

- Feeling inadequate or worthless: If your partner makes you feel as if you are not good enough or that you should be lucky that he or she puts up with you, this is a very clear sign of manipulation. A manipulative partner will try to make you feel as worthless or inadequate as possible so that you don't feel as if you could do any better. Rather than make the effort to be a loving and enjoyable partner that you would never want to leave, he or she instead chooses to put you down beneath his or her level so that you will be afraid to leave.

- Having difficulties expressing your thoughts and emotions: perhaps at the beginning, you tried to express your honest thoughts and emotions or perhaps you always had these difficulties. In either case, if you find it difficult to express yourself openly to your partner or you feel as if you don't even know how to begin; you are probably in a manipulative relationship. Your partner makes you feel like a nag for expressing yourself.

In a healthy relationship, your partner would encourage you to express yourself and make sure that he or she is always aware of how you feel.

- Feeling insecure: whether you are afraid your partner could leave you at any moment or you are afraid of how your partner might act, feelings of insecurity have no place in a relationship. In all the nonstop stress and chaos of the world, your relationship should be that one safe haven in which you can retreat to feel safe and secure. If your relationship with your partner does not feel like such a safe place, his or her manipulative behavior is likely the cause of that insecurity.

- Having difficulties saying no: if your partner makes you feel guilty or ashamed for saying no to any of his or her requests to the point that you rarely, if ever, say no, this is not healthy. A loving partner will respect your boundaries and your wishes. If he or she tries to make you do something regardless of how you feel about it, he or she is manipulative. And if you have difficulty saying no to your partner, you are definitely being manipulated.

- Feeling afraid: you find yourself spending more time afraid of losing your partner than you do actually enjoying his or her presence. You are afraid of your partner abandoning you. You may even be afraid of what will happen next time he or she loses their temper. Such fear is toxic in a relationship. You cannot form a genuine and loving bond with each other if you have such fear in the way. So if your partner is using fear to control you, he or she does not love you, no matter what he or she says.

Read through both lists of signs a few times so that you have them clearly in your head. Think about your relationship carefully and figure out which signs you can see in your partner and in yourself. It is hard work to recognize when you are being manipulated but if you are truly honest with yourself, you will be able to figure it out. So be as honest with yourself as you possibly can (you can do it, you don't have to be afraid of your own reaction as you do with your partner).

Arenas For Delusion

We know manipulation can take many forms. For those who choose to manipulate, using the essential elements of life to exercise manipulation may prove tempting. When something is essential to your subsistence, it presents the opportunity for manipulation to take place because life may be difficult (for some unbearable) without it. Below we will examine some of the common areas of life that partners manipulate.

Financial Manipulation

One of the most obvious ways to detect the presence of manipulation in a relationship is to examine the role money plays. We live in a capitalistic society; hence, money does indeed equal power, and this may also be true in relationships. Usually when the manipulative mate tends to be the primary breadwinner, you can be sure that money will be used to gain leverage in the relationship. More often than not, money will; furthermore, this can include the withholding of money to punish or persuade a partner, and be used to control the behavior of their partner. Even in relationships where both partners have independent incomes, the one with more money will often assume a more powerful position. Money is a powerful tool for manipulators because it is absolutely essential for survival. However, when money is used to manipulate a partner it is usually preceded by psychological manipulation.

The psychological component must be employed first in order for the financial component to work. The manipulated partner must come to believe that they "need" the manipulator's money. They must believe that their manipulative mate is providing for them in a manner that another will not, or that it will be difficult to obtain another partner who will provide at the same or higher standard. The manipulated partner comes to believe that the manipulative partner is a superior provider even if he or she is only providing the basic essentials needed for daily living. The manipulative partner does not necessarily have to be providing at an exceptional level, rather the manipulated partner must only be convinced that they cannot provide as well for themselves.

To the contrary, the primary breadwinner may also be manipulated when the partner makes the receipt of money the basis for the relationship. They may employ their own techniques to undermine their mate by psychologically and financially abusing them. To begin with, they may put down the amount their partner earns, insisting their mate could and should earn more. Or that he or she could have had a wealthier mate but chose to be with them out of love. They may even demand money to remain in the relationship.

Another type of financial manipulation occurs when a partner tries to dissuade their mate from seeking greater financial opportunities for fear that they will leave for a presumably better romantic prospect, once they are in a more desirable financial position. Financial manipulation of this type may also include a desire to have a partner remain in a financially dependent position. Examples of this includes preventing a partner from making a substantial financial contribution to the household, or encouraging them to stay in a lower paying position by discouraging them from applying for better paying positions, or seeking higher education. All of this is done with the goal of keeping their partner financially needy and more likely to remain in the relationship. Again, there is an obvious self-esteem component present because the manipulative party is operating out of their own sense of insecurity as well as their partner's. This type of manipulation, like all types of manipulation, is rooted in issues of self-worth.

Another popular way in which financial manipulation occurs is through the act of what we call radical appreciation. This occurs when one exaggerates the financial contributions of their mate. The manipulative partner does this so that their significant other begins to expect praise for what they provide, and consequently starts to define their identity by their ability to do so. They develop a need to be seen as an excellent provider above all else. The type of adoration given by a partner who engages in radical appreciation is not genuine, and is established as a tool for manipulation. The extreme appreciation is shown so that lavish gifts will continue to be given while extreme disdain will likely be displayed if they are not. Thus, the manipulated mate will become so concerned with providing and being viewed as a good provider, they will never question the requests of their partner, no matter how extravagant. This occurs because they have developed a need to maintain their status and image as breadwinner/provider in order to preserve their self-esteem.

This is dangerous because when this partner tries to honor requests for which they really do not have the financial means, they may become fiscally overwhelmed. Often this is how the cycle of debt begins. When it comes to financial manipulation, which strategy is employed is irrelevant. After all, the ultimate goal of the manipulator is to diminish the humanity of their partner by reducing them into someone whose worth is attached to something outside of their value as a human being.

Sexual Manipulation

Sexual manipulation in a relationship occurs when a partner uses sex as a means to achieve a desired result or action from their partner. The most common type of sexual manipulation is the pressuring of a partner to have sex in exchange for something else. And this something else could literally be anything as long as it is significant to the person being manipulated. Likewise, it is also common for a partner to withhold sex until their mate relents and honors a request, expectation, or demand.

Sexual manipulation within relationships is dangerous because it diminishes the reasons why sex should be a feature of healthy romantic unions. Intimacy should provide each partner with a safe environment in which to experience pleasure, foster a sense of closeness and trust, and promote fidelity. When sexual manipulation occurs it creates pathways for feelings of insecurity, abuse, insignificance, and anger to develop.

Once a partner begins to feel this way, they will likely seek ways to lessen those negative feelings which may include reciprocating manipulative behaviors with their partner, infidelity, or ending the relationship. Sexual manipulation can be avoided if both parties establish the role that sex will play early in the relationship. How is this done? By having any honest conversation about sexual habits, preferences, needs, concerns, and expectations. Couples should clearly define what they can and cannot tolerate, and what they expect when it comes to sex as it relates to other issues within the relationship.

If having a partner who wants to have sex even if you are angry with them is a problem for you, you need to say that. If you believe that you are entitled to sex whenever you want it because________________ (fill in your blank). Then you need to say that. If you are only willing to have sex under certain conditions then you need to tell your partner why you feel that way and what those conditions are.

The goal here is not to persuade your mate to let one of you take charge of your sex life. The goal is to make sure that your other half is informed, and to determine if what they expect sexually is in conflict with what you expect sexually. There is no moral judgment call as to what is right and what is wrong (with the exception of sexual abuse—that is always wrong), only what works for you as a couple. Discuss your expectations so that you can avoid miscommunication and circumvent manipulation. Now that we have looked at some of the areas in which manipulation occurs, we will examine how manipulation may be stopped.

Chapter 3 Methods of mind control

There are numerous methods of mind control, and here you locate a fast outline of the absolute most normal ones. Hope never to observe the world with similar eyes after you read this part - because you will take a gander at numerous components of your regular reality with different eyes. When you comprehend what the methods of mind control are, you will all around rapidly perceive the amount it has turned into a piece of regular day to day existences as of now.

Companion Group Pressure

This is one of the most well-known methods that is being used. Furthermore, it is one that is naturally being used by adolescent possess as of now. Everyone wants to have a place with a specific group of people, a particular "clan." When the group that you wish to have a place with (or just the predominant group) weights you to change your assessment, think a specific way or do a particular thing, there is a high probability that you would do and think feels that you wouldn't do or think without anyone else.

Disinhibition

During the time spent socialization, when we grew up, we as a whole learned not to pursue each conduct motivation we have. We secure and refine the capacity to reflect and settle on conscious decisions. In any case, there are methods to fix this sort of hindrance.

Reciting or Singing

Indeed, such innocuous things like reciting or singing can be used as a type of mind control. Furthermore, consider it - numerous religious networks use some reciting or singing to fortify the people's connection to their group.

Pacing and driving

This is most effectively done in one-on-one compulsion. Specific language and standards of conduct from the objective person are grabbed and "reflected." Numerous people think it is essentially a parroting or replicating a person's words or body developments, yet so as to be viable, it must be done much progressively unpretentious. If done right, it made the subconscious recognition that both of you are in order, and the other person will feel as though you genuinely get the person in question and thus will trust and like you. At that point, you can begin the main part - basically controlling where the discussion is going.

Dress Codes

Honestly, even school uniforms. There are numerous valid justifications for dress codes, yet one that not many people are deliberately mindful of is that it decreases a person's uniqueness and rather underlines his having a place with a group

- therefore making it almost sure that the individual will act as per the group. It is somewhat similar to the inborn skin works of art that have been used by the precursors amid war.

None of these methods of mind control is terrible all by itself. It just depends on what ultimate objective it is being used. There are a lot more methods of mind control. For the most part, all alone, their mental power is restricted, yet when joined with one another, they make a ground-breaking manipulative force.

The Best Mind Control Techniques

Authority: The best of the pioneers most likely knows the best of the mind control techniques. Take a gander at them - they are so well known. Wouldn't you say that they can control people's minds? Give it an idea - better, have a similar outlook as a pioneer does.

Fixation: The people who can control their mind well are the top representatives, pioneers, and sportspersons to give some examples of groups. What they, without a doubt, share for all intents and purpose is a method by which they can control their minds. If it weren't for that, they would not have been the place they are today. Fixation and center are the key.

Champ: Think as a victor does. They don't dread losing - they take it essentially as a piece of the more noteworthy expectation to absorb information. A victor is the best person you'd at any point seen. Be a victor.

Inspirational Attitude: This is significant because except if you have it, you don't have a clue how to do it. The more you're uninformed, the more you become inclined to turning into a disappointment.

Exercise: Most people think wrongly that if they eat well and focus on what they are doing, they can achieve anything they desire. In any case, the significant point is that if they are unfitting themselves - they can't take a walk for the endeavor. Practicing your mind and body is of most extreme significance.

Yoga: Finally, these hundreds of years old all-inescapable information of Yoga is what is required if you need supreme control over your mind. It utilizes the most scientific stances and 'kriyas' that will enable you to consummate the mind control techniques.

It is all in mind - it's anything but a prominent commercial trick. It is a procedure that each individual must experience.

Utilizing Hypnosis Mind Control on Yourself And Others

One thing that permits hypnosis mind control to stand out from other methods that people use to reconstruct their subconscious mind is that it isn't restricted on who it very well may be used by. Hypnosis mind control can effectively be used on yourself, yet it can likewise be used similarly as successfully on others. Be that as it may, before you can use hypnosis mind control on yourself or others, you should have an essential comprehension of how the subconscious mind works and what techniques work best with hypnosis mind control.

Some portion of seeing how the subconscious mind works is understanding what it is. The subconscious mind is the piece of your mind that handles and controls certain musings and activities, for the most part, the silly ones. Your subconscious mind is accountable for the majority of your sentiments, and regardless of how hard you may take a stab at subduing, any of your emotions is practically unimaginable. Be that as it may, if you realize how to effectively use hypnosis mind control you will most likely impact your subconscious mind, which will give you control over the majority of your emotions, yet can likewise enable you to influence others. Probably the best thing about utilizing hypnosis mind control on yourself and others is that the techniques you would use on others are similar ones that you would use on yourself.

One inquiry that numerous people pose to when it comes to utilizing these techniques is if they are protected to use. The response to this inquiry is that if they are used appropriately and for the right reasons they are consummately protected to use, in truth numerous experts use hypnosis as a method for helping people achieve their objectives. For instance, someone who has had a go at everything to quit smoking may experience hypnosis as a last method for bringing an end to the negative behavior pattern. What the specialist is doing is utilizing hypnosis mind control to impact that person's subconscious mind to enable them to quit smoking.

With hypnosis mind control the main thing that must be cultivated, regardless of whether it is for yourself or another person, is they should be in a relaxed state; however, they additionally must focus on something to help keep them relaxed. Perhaps the most significant confusion that people have with hypnosis is that people who are under hypnosis are sleeping. The fact of the matter is with hypnosis people are entirely wakeful, yet they are loose to such an extent that any proposals that are made can enter the subconscious mind effortlessly.

Perhaps the best thing about utilizing hypnosis mind control on yourself or others is the way effective it is. If you converse with anyone who has experienced any hypnosis, you will catch wind of how it has transformed them. Hypnosis can be used to modify people's impression of themselves or even change how they think. When a person is in that completely relaxed state, the recommendations that are being made should be altered depending on what one would like to achieve. For instance, if you put yourself into a sleep-inducing state to help modify how you consider yourself once in the relaxed state, you will need to tune in to tapes that send a positive message about yourself.

Notwithstanding, while hypnosis mind control can be advantageous, it additionally has a few defeats. Before utilizing hypnosis on yourself or others, you will need to discover increasingly about the impediments to guarantee you are settling on the right decision. A most exceedingly terrible aspect concerning hypnosis is that sure people abuse it, they use it to get others to do things that aren't right, or they use it to trick these people out of something. Be that as it may, when the right people use it for the right reasons, it is perhaps the best apparatus around.

Hypnosis mind control is alright for anyone to use, no enduring damage should be possible to yourself or others, as long as it is used for the right reasons. Hypnosis should be possible by pretty much anyone who knows how however if there are not kidding issues that should be managed it is prescribed to see a hypnotherapist because of how quick they can venture into your subconscious mind.

Proper language utilization is one of the top 5 persuasive speech presentation components. Adjectives can include hues while giving a sales speech or presentation. By utilizing a straightforward memory stunt, the list of most generally used adjectives can be recalled while speaking to the leads/customers or drafting a persuasive sales letter.

BEST abbreviation condenses persuasive adjectives list:

Best

Simple

Basic

Top

Use the Word "Best" to Write a Good Letter of Recommendation

List of adjectives that begin with B- - positive words:

Beautiful

Brilliant

Better

Give Speeches Easily by Using the Word "Simple"

Nearly everybody concurs that the significance of public speaking is to induce the lead. Most persuasive speeches will have this word "Simple" make intrigue and want. Although there are many different words for the word "Simple, for example, inconvenience free, easy, effortless, laid-back, and unproblematic, it still runs the universe of public speaking as it is straightforward.

One more list of spellbinding adjectives that begin with E

Exquisite

Erratic (Unconventional)

How to Give a Good Sales Presentation? Use the Word "Basic"

Giving excellent presentations include potent words and reasonable utilization of language. The word "Basic" is one of the most powerful words in the English language, which is an equivalent word for ease and straightforwardness.

Adjectives starting with S:

Savvy

Sweet

Depicting words that begin with T:

Tuneful

Too

Both, while composing and speaking, utilizing the right words gets greater clarity and accuracy in the discussion, which is one of the components of collaboration skills. To use the right words, one must recollect the jargon with the goal that it is promptly in the brain and can be used precipitously. Mental helpers are probably the ideal approaches to remember and keep the data in the long haul memory. BEST is one such mental aide's models that help salespersons to recall the most broadly used adjectives in the English language. This list of persuasive adjectives will come conveniently during business sales presentations and persuasive speeches. Most importantly, it takes just a couple of moments to recall these most regular adjectives- - BEST.

There are sure words that can be persuasive, or notwithstanding compelling! Use these words, and your composition will deliver a higher amount of what you desire...the reader making the move you have set before them.

Here is a list of powerful, persuasive words you should use when writing to persuade your reader to make a move:

simple, good, best, spared, guaranteed, demonstrated, cash, sheltered, new, improved, results, claim, free, you, your, opportunity, wellbeing, venture, love, revelation, certified, genuine feelings of serenity, budgetary security, envision, bother free, restore, revive, reevaluate, in a flash, ace, amplify, catch, vanquish, characterize, convert, make, cancel, keep away from, help, manufacture, copy, break, rouse, survive, benefit, simplify, tackle, change, release, win, touch off, produce, center, because, quick, rebate, restricted

Whew, a significant list! There are a lot more power words that will enable you to compose with influence, read any sales copy you find, for much more thoughts.

When composing a persuasive piece use the same number of these persuasive words as you can fit in the progression of your composition. They shouldn't sound ungainly, or as they don't have a place. Your composing ought to consistently stream and sound natural...you know, similar to your conversing with a companion or relative.

Persuasive Words That Convert and Sell

The object of the game in the Internet advertising business is to make sales. One of the best methods for creating sales is using a sales page. Most sales pages convert about 1% if the total page sees into sales. If your sales page is changing over at a rate much lower than 1%, you most likely need to make a few changes. One of the best moves that you can make is adding increasingly persuasive words to your sales copy. The best sales pages make exceptionally viable use of these persuasive words.

So what are these secretive words that convince? An investigation done at a noteworthy University has identified 12 words that people react to. The initial five words have to do with essential human wants. Wants are enthusiastic needs and needs that are always prepared to react to something.

These words, when people are presented to them, register with their feelings, and nearly urge them to focus and react. The initial five are Health, Love, Money, Safety, and Save. Utilizing any of these words when portraying the advantages of your item will draw the reader's consideration because of their passionate intrigue.

The examination additionally found that people like to encounter new thoughts, ideas. Furthermore, for reasons unknown, the terms: New, Discovery, and Breakthrough are exceptionally persuasive words. These words ought to be used in the main section or two of your sales piece to interest your reader and propel him to peruse on.

Other persuasive terms instill a conviction that all is good and believability in the reader. These terms are Easy, Guarantee, and Proven. These persuasive words can instill a sense of trust in your reader.

The last persuasive word that makes a list is the word, You. The best sales copy converses with the reader as though he were an old companion. Successive use of the word 'you' makes the reader feel pleasant and quiet. When making any buy, everybody needs to recognize how might this benefit them. By telling them in an agreeable, casual, well-disposed style, your reader is substantially more liable to make that buy and snap on that 'purchase' button.

So if your sales pages aren't changing over just as you trusted, have a go at utilizing these persuasive words that are demonstrated to change over and sell.

Enchantment Persuasive Words With Great Persuasion Power That Can Bring You Instant Riches and Success

Enchantment Persuasive Word 1: Safe

Why It's Powerful?

This wellbeing needs to manifest themselves in such things as an inclination for professional stability, the need for having bank accounts, they need protection strategies to secure relatives and secret stash to be used for crisis circumstances. We can reason that people esteem wellbeing more than anything else. So when you notice the word "safe" in your correspondence, automatically it'll make an individual to offer need to what you're stating. This is one of the most potent persuasive words that can without much of a stretch impact or persuade somebody to say "YES" to you.

Enchantment Persuasive Word 2: New

Why It's Powerful?

It'll make people inquisitive and eager to comprehend what new things, thoughts, and tips are there for them. This word could be one of the most potent persuasive composition words. In any case, if you've disillusioned the people around you beforehand, perhaps they won't be intrigued to hear what's going on from you. The key here is to convey over and surpass the people's desires consistently. When they've related you with incredible stuff and see you as an individual who'll always surpass their desires, they'll like to work together or hear something new from you once more.

Enchantment Persuasive Word 3: Love

Why It's Powerful?

As should be obvious, one of human's essential needs is to give and get love. Usually, people partner to love with embraces from guardians, kisses from spouses and time went through with beloved relatives. For your data, love is a passionate word. It speaks to a condition of constructive feeling that people will show to other people around them. When you notice the word love, automatically they'll relate the word with something positive in their brain and bring them into an enthusiastic minute. As scientific research and studies are gradually demonstrating that feelings will result in general break an individual's logic harshly, it'll make that individual progressively defenseless against be influenced.

Powerful Persuasive Words That Guarantee Profits

Regardless of whether you understand it or not, making a buy, passionate action. This implies, generally, you purchase stuff because it makes you feel better. That new car smells decent, and you look good in it. The new extra-large flat-screen TV makes you glad when you see those enormous, intense pictures on the screen (and it might even intrigue the neighbors). To put it, when you peruse among various sale things, you are pulled in to the item that makes you feel the best.

A thing for the nursery may be bought because it would look extraordinary as a feature of your arranging. You buy that front room set because it feels so comfortable and comfortable and looks fabulous in your parlor. The car you are thinking about looks good and smells extraordinary. The car organizations are not dumb. That new car smell isn't something normal; the maker intentionally adds that smell to improve sales. Why do you imagine that all new cars smell the equivalent? Without acknowledging it, people purchase things for enthusiastic motivations to fulfill their passionate needs.

Certain powerful, persuasive words fulfill these enthusiastic needs more than others. By utilizing these persuasive words in your titles, advertisements, messages, features, and sales pages, you can all the more effectively influence people to purchase and nearly guarantee profits.

Utilizing robust, persuasive words can improve your outcomes significantly. Following is a rundown of powerful, persuasive words. Use them in your titles, advertisements, messages, features, and sales pages to naturally guarantee profits.

- Astonishing
- Declaring
- Bonus
- Breakthrough
- Advantageous
- Markdown
- Find
- Simple

- Restrictive

- Exceptional

- Quick

- Free

- Guarantee

- Significant

- Increment

- Amazing

- New

- Presently

- Exceptional

- Powerful

- Benefit

- Demonstrated

- Amazing

- Deal

- Mystery

Protection

How to identify a manipulative persuader

Besides learning how to manipulate or persuade people to doing what you want it is important to know how to spot and stop manipulative persuaders. First, we have to acknowledge that manipulation and control fit right into the current world. People use media, power and even interpersonal relationships to get what they want. We have to admit that everyone has used some form of manipulation at one point or the other. In fact, we encounter masters of manipulations severally, without even realizing it.

Manipulation has been linked to forms of emotional blackmail. Master manipulators use certain behaviors to make us feel, think, and act in a particular way even without noticing. In effect, we end up doing what the manipulator wants. And that is the main problem with manipulation- that we end up changing our behaviors. Most times, we end up taking the bait, hook, line, and sinker, thus allowing the manipulator to get away with it.

The basic manipulation tool is normally words. If you can master the use of words, it becomes easy to control people. Interestingly, master manipulators are so good at what they do that you have to be on the lookout in order to spot them. Below are some of the ways you can identify a manipulator.

1. The manipulators fake concern and make you talk

This is normally the first step of a master manipulator. As mentioned earlier, manipulation works best where there is trust. The manipulator will make you trust him/her by sharing some information that seems personal and intimate. You are more likely to share information about yourself in exchange. This manipulator is looking for your strengths and weaknesses, what you love, what you hate, what can be used against you, your desires, and any other information they can use. Another term for this technique is reconnaissance, which is, surveying.

2. They are too good at talking in almost all subjects and will change the topic if it does not suit them.

The art of language is very important to all of us but more so to manipulators. A master manipulator must be well skilled in all forms of communication, that is, verbal, facial, and body language. To catch your attention, this person will use fluid and flowery language and will always have a witty and surprising argument in store even if it is built on lies. For instance, he/she can say, "you look like a duckling that dull dress". If you look offended by the comment, he/she will add "I did not know that you cannot take a joke." That is a win-win for them; first, they have expressed their opinion and second, they have found a way to get out of the otherwise ugly situation. Before you can even confront them, these manipulators change the topic and talk about things that have no connection to the topic at hand.

3. They are almost always charming

Basically, manipulators know that being pleasant and wonderful makes most people fall into manipulation traps. After all, you have to first stroke the horse you intend to ride. That is why most sales and marketing people are so sweet even when you are mean to them. They know you will gradually fall for the charm. Master manipulators are very entertaining and will make you think they have such an exciting life. Their tastes will always be good and will always pay attention to your needs. You will feel understood when they are around. That is the first step- to make you feel important, wanted, and greats- a big and essential part of their life.

Next, these persons will start manipulating you with all the charm. The net of seduction they threw around you ensures that you do not evaluate situations effectively. You will see everything they do through good light. Even when you have doubts, the manipulator will have known you so well that he/she makes you change your mind immediately.

4. They will use sarcasm to hurt you

As mentioned earlier, a manipulator knows how to manipulate words. If there is anything he/she will avoid its direct communication. Instead of calling you a dog, these people will give you a bone. So, instead of directly challenging your thoughts, they will use sarcasm to minimize the value of your feelings, thoughts, and actions and also ridicule you. Master manipulators want to make their victims feel inferior and insecure. For instance, you can notice some nastiness in their communications. A statement such as "Maybe you should read a little more so that you can have distinguished friends" could mean "You are very stupid and that is why you don't have any classy friends." Because of the trust, you might see this as a sincere comment meant to help you become better. Know this, a person who wants to help you will use sincere and direct communication. Not some hidden jargons. Furthermore, a person with sincere intentions will not devalue you or your friends, instead, he/she will offer concrete advice.

5.   Master manipulators subtly threaten you

Manipulators are also known for using indirect threats. From very influential leaders to small domestic manipulators, anyone who uses master manipulation techniques applies threats in some cases. Normally, these threats involve making your worst fears appear valid. For instance, a person can say "If you keep treating me like that I will definitely stop giving you this support." Or, "if you keep feeding like that, you will not fit into your wedding gown". Simply, this person is making you feel insecure and stay right where you are so that they can have power over you.

Maybe this person is bothered by how happy you are when you meet that friend or eat that piece of cake. And instead of telling you about it directly, they would rather use indirect communication. A person who is genuinely concerned will ask you about it directly.

6.   The guilt-trip you

When dealing with a manipulator, you might realize feelings of guilt for unexplained reasons. A person who uses manipulation techniques will consistently victimize you and make you feel like you are the victimizer. For instance, if you turn the request of this person down, he/she will remind you of that bad childhood experience that leads him/her to this situation and you are not helping. This manipulator will also use past experiences to justify their wrongdoings. They might say that there is a curse in the family, or someone mistreated them, or their life is full of bad omen, et cetera. While normal people will not talk about their bad past experiences with pride, manipulators will seem to enjoy talking about it and eve blaming it for the current situation.

For instance, if you have a spouse who ignores your needs every time and you call him /her out, he/she will respond with something like; "Are you angry because I am not attentive? Do you know that I deal with a father who ignored me since I was 3 years old? Can you not at least handle your own needs like me? " This person will say this with such pride that you end up feeling useless, disarmed and too self-centered. After all, how can you criticize someone who has experienced such trauma?

7. They are self-appointed judges and advisers of your life

Have you ever found that there is someone who is always advising and guiding you but you do to know how they got that power? This person seems to want to intervene in every one of your situations with or without your permission. Manipulators are very good at telling you how to live your life yet theirs is a problem. In fact, you might notice that a person is advising you to proverbially drink water while they are drinking wine. Additionally, this person will give you advice and even quote a great philosophical maxim to support it. He/she has a step by step guide on how you should be doing this and that. If you do not follow their advice, they will wait for that opportunity to tell you "You see, that is the result of not listening to me." Again, if you follow that advice and fail, they will say "you did not follow my advice word for word." Either way, you will be the one to take the blame.

A good adviser will not dictate to you what to do then blame you latter if you fail. Instead, he/she will give you honest advice and leave you to make a choice. A person who genuinely cares for you will want you to be free and not dependent.

8. A manipulator will happily blame you

A manipulative person will always blame you even when they are on the wrong. For instance, If a wife caught his husband cheating and made the accusation, the husband will yell at her angrily accusing her of not being there when needed and also snooping and spying on him. This man might go into a long rant of why he feels that the wife does not trust him, that all relationships are built on trust and the probably mention that the wife is ever busy. In the end, the wife will feel responsible for the actions of the husband and even apologize for being absent and controlling.

9. A manipulative person will try to make you indebted to him/her.

Majority of us will feel indebted to someone who showed kindness in moments of need. The statement "I owe you one" was coined from this feeling. In fact, a number of people will pay back tenfold. Manipulators know that indebt-ness can be used as leverage. So, they will help you out and then ask for a favor in return. If you turn them down, they will remind you of that help they offered, even if it was years ago. IN most cases, you will realize that the help they offered does not equate the favor they are asking for. For instance, a person might have offered you a ride home, then two days later, he/she comes asking for $200.

Not to say that every person offering you helps is a manipulator but, it is important to be on the lookout. Some of these people have motives behind their "oh so dear" help. It will help you turn down any help which you feel will come with a price tag.

If your gut is telling you that a person you trust is manipulating you, do not ignore. You might be onto something, even if it does not look like it yet. Yes, that person might be genuinely concerned about your welfare or he/she wants to really know you. However, if you sense that this person is avoiding direct questions, trying to induce a slip of the tongue, is treating you like a specimen, then it is time to either run or hit the stop button on them.

Know that knowledge cannot be altered, facts cannot be changed, but beliefs can be manipulated. If you have some strong beliefs, make a point of guarding them consciously and closely. If a manipulative person knows them, he/she will know how to manipulate you. Those people who are very outspoken about their beliefs such as missionaries, motivational speakers and visionary leaders also have facts to support them. These people are extra sure of what they are talking about.

You might be thinking that you are well armed with information to support your beliefs but a master manipulator will find a way to manipulate you. The best protection you can use is to measure your words. Measure your beliefs through the eyes of others. For instance, you can ask yourself, "What your spouse think or say if he/she knew about that particular belief?" Who id your audience and how can they perceive your life? What is their goal in life and how much would their betrayal affect you?

Besides the use of words, assess the other ways through which you express yourself.

-	What does your body language say about you?

-	What about your facial expression?

-	That tone of voice you use? Does it betray you?

-	What about your presence?

A master manipulator will pick a lot from your verbal communication, and even more from other forms of expression. Your eyes can easily give you away. The tone of your voice can easily tell someone about emotions you are trying to hide.

If you do not have emotional intelligence, the manipulators will easily learn your traits and know the buttons they can push. Emotional intelligence is defined as the capability of a person to recognize his/her own emotions and those of others, to spot the difference between different types of emotions and label them in the right way, to use the appropriate emotional information to guide behavior and thinking patterns, and to adjust or manage emotions to achieve goals and fit in different environments.

Simply put, emotional intelligence involves recognizing the emotions you are feeling when talking to different people and using that awareness to protect yourself and guide your actions so that a manipulator cannot pick a lot from your tone of voice, body language eye contact, et cetera. Truth be told, acquiring emotional intelligence is not an easy thing. It can be a bit of a learning curve but at least, being aware of your emotions is a good starting point. Another practice that can help you giving the manipulator too much information is setting some specific, well-defined goals that will help you take control of your actions and achieve what you want.

Chapter 4 Characteristics of manipulators

Manipulators take manipulation seriously. They often treat scheming as if their lives depend upon it because they believe their lives do. They honestly believe that if they do not deceive and exploit their partner, their life and well-being will be adversely affected. This belief is usually deep-seated, and formed early in the life of the manipulator. It is quite common that manipulators learned this behavior from a parent or significant other. Those who grew up seeing manipulation in the relationships of the adults in their lives may be more likely to act based upon ulterior motives. Why? Because they understand how deception works.

People learn the strategies employed in the governing of relationships from the adults in their lives, most notably their parents. Just as those who grow up seeing their parents interact in a healthy positive relationship are more likely to construct and conduct their relationship using that model, the manipulator will likely model their relationship after the first significant romantic relationship they observed.

Also, as we mentioned earlier, many manipulators have been involved in relationships where they were manipulated. They can vividly recall feeling powerless within a romantic relationship. They remember doing everything they could to please a manipulative partner, who in their view rarely acknowledged and never appreciated anything they did. In turn, they decided that since someone is destined to be the lesser in a relationship, it would not be them, not ever again. Therefore, any perceived slight or disobedience ignites a need to get even or oppress their partner into doing their will. This is done with the goal of making sure the partner does not act independently, for independence is the enemy of a controlling partner.

While manipulation is time consuming and may be emotionally draining, the manipulator is reluctant to discontinue its use because they have become addicted to the feeling of security, no matter how false, it can bring. The manipulator engages in acts of manipulation because it helps them feel as if the relationship, as well as their partner, is under control. Opposition ceases to concern the manipulator, and really becomes just another hurdle that they have effectively developed the strategies to overcome. It is an odd sort of confidence that a manipulator has. While born of insecurity, master manipulators know how to inspire their partner into a desired behavior or action.

Ironically, manipulators lack true genuine self-confidence. This is because a great deal of their false self-esteem comes from their ability to control their partner, and that esteem is jeopardized every single time their partner acts independently. A key factor in stopping manipulation is gaining control over the only person you can truly control: yourself. This is as true for the person being manipulated as it is for the manipulator. To do this, the decision to work towards gaining authentic self-confidence must be made. All of your focus must be directed on accepting what makes you unique and doing what makes you happy. There must be a willingness to do the work necessary to become the type of person you most admire. Be forewarned; this is an arduous task. You will be required to confront those aspects of your development and personality which may invoke feelings of shame, anger, guilt, and sadness. But those are the very feelings that contributed to becoming involved in a relationship characterized by manipulation because those issues were never successfully resolved.

And remember, time is the enemy of those involved in manipulative relationships. Why? Because for the manipulator, the time spent puppeteering a partner is time lost forever. The time you spent destroying your relationship, when you could have been strengthening it, will not return. Time you used to learn how to deceive and hurt your partner, could have been spent learning to understand and support them. And it is time that is completely wasted should your partner decide to do the work they need to do in order to heal, because once they heal, they may decide to leave you. All that time spent manipulating only to end up old, lonely, and bitter.

For the person being manipulated, time is not your friend either. The longer it takes you to assert and save yourself, the more jaded and insecure you will become. You will forget how to be in a healthy relationship, and you may even lose the desire for one. After all, you were the puppet. Without someone to pull your strings, you may be utterly lost. So as time passes, you too will become older, woefully bitter, and less trusting of others as well as yourself. Sadly, you will eventually settle into your status as victim. Who knows, maybe your manipulator will get healthy and dump you. All that time you spent allowing yourself to be manipulated for the sake of your "chess game" relationship was wasted. When it is over, all you will have left is a bruised and battle scarred soul, and possibly some really confused children who have no clue as to what a healthy relationship should look like because you never showed them one. It is then that you will likely realize that you could have done something radically different.

Deceptive Liaisons

Emotions abide with every breathe we take. Likewise, emotions are affected by past experiences. Our feelings during experiences impact how we learn the difference between good and bad feelings. We all want to feel good. Yet when we become accustomed to living in negative environments and interacting with toxic people, we can have trouble discerning between good feelings and bad feelings. Think about people who do really bad things, but they actually feel good while they are doing them. If we do not learn how to appropriately process emotions, the result can be failure to adequately address situations in an effort to avoid bad feelings. Negativity can permeate our relationships;

consequently, if we do not recognize it as such, negativity will never cease. Furthermore, when we ignore sound reasoning and only concentrate on our feelings, it can be difficult to detach from even the unhealthiest of relationships. Indeed, a manipulator will even use your fear of negative emotions to control you. For example, consider the case of a client we will call *Richard. Richard had been involved with *Shelia for about a year and a half. Richard has two children, a son and a daughter from his first marriage. In the beginning of the relationship, Shelia behaved as if she were interested in becoming close with his children. She regularly bought the children gifts, and she and Richard would spend time together with the kids. Shelia eventually gained the trust of the children and they began to confide in her.

As time went on, Richard proposed to Shelia and she accepted. After they were married, it was decided that the children would live with Richard and Shelia. At first, things seemed great. Richard started coming home earlier to spend time with Shelia and the children. Then Shelia mentioned that she no longer felt they had enough time alone. Richard decided to make every Friday night their date night. Initially Shelia seemed happy about this. However, she soon began to feel that their date night was not enough, and she again told Richard how she felt. Richard tried to find more time to spend with Shelia; however, because he owned his own business and had to care for his aging parents, he did not always have time to spare.

Shelia then began to pick fights with Richard and she would yell that she felt like a babysitter, and could not understand why she had to suffer and be alone when she was a faithful spouse. Unlike a cheating whore who betrayed her husband by possibly getting pregnant by another man; Richard's first marriage had ended due to his first wife's infidelity, and issues surrounding the paternity of their last child. She would then remind Richard that there are not many women who, with her good looks, education and background, would take a chance on a divorced, middle-aged man with two children, one of whom is disabled.

Richard could remember how his life was before Shelia, and how lonely and unhappy he was. He remembered wishing that a good woman would come into his life and love him and his children. He truly believed Shelia was this woman. Deep down he felt lucky because he thought Shelia could have probably married better. Shelia knew this and she used it to make Richard feel guilty. His guilt would usually prompt him to do things to try and please her.

Sometimes this involved his taking care of her needs and wants before the needs of his children. Even worse, he and Shelia developed the habit of badmouthing his first wife in front of his children. He did this to demonstrate his appreciation for the good Shelia, and to show solidarity with her. Neither bothered to consider the affect that speaking badly about the mother of his children may have on his kids' mental and emotional health.

Is Shelia being manipulative? How has Richard's fear of experiencing loneliness influenced his susceptibility to be manipulated? This example may seem a bit extreme, but for many people this is reality. There are people involved in "everyday" relationships where manipulation is a constant feature. To further illustrate manipulation in relationships, examine a less traditional romantic entanglement; the type of snare that people are slow to acknowledge but it is, nevertheless, quite common.

*Dawn is a student in law school. Dawn had been working as a waitress, and barely made enough money to pay her rent and buy food. Additionally, the expenses associated with her earning a law degree are significant. At the urging of a friend, Dawn decided to become involved with a much older married man because he offered financial assistance. At first, Dawn told herself that she would only be with this man until she found a better job, and could support herself without a suitor's assistance. Instead, Dawn lost her job and has had a great deal of trouble finding a new one. She has also had some unexpected school related expenses.

As a result of her involvement with this man, she has become isolated from her friends. Also she is reluctant to date a young student in one of her classes who is interested in her because she says she is afraid that he cannot afford to help her. She has not even considered that they share similar interests and goals. In truth, she has internalized the belief that she could not function in a "normal" relationship anymore. Moreover, Dawn's "sugar daddy" is very demanding and verbally insults her regularly.

When he fears she may be contemplating exiting the relationship, he calls her names like "whore" and "slut." He often tells her that she will never find another man to do all he does for her, and that she will be the world's dumbest lawyer. He also regularly reminds her that without him she would have nothing, for that is what she had before she met him. Strangely enough, he then threatens to cut her off, and tells her that she is going to have to start taking care of herself. He also makes it clear to her that the needs of his wife and young children come first. Whenever he does this she starts to panic because she has developed a belief that without him she would be helpless.

Imagine a young woman who is one of the top students in her class, who used to enjoy taking care of herself and valued her independence, a young woman who loved being around people, now feels helpless. Her days are spent catering to the needs of a middle-aged man who is unwilling to fully commit to her or the family he created. Dawn began her relationship looking to use someone for her own gain, but this has backfired monumentally. The relationship that was supposed to give her independence has instead made her dependent. The relationship that was supposed to make her feel sexy and desirable instead makes her feel disgusting and unattractive. The trips, gifts, and admiration that characterized the relationship in the beginning have been replaced by social isolation, faultfinding, and incessant bargaining for even the most basic of goods. Dawn tells herself that she is better off than she was, but she knows she has paid an exceptionally high price for a security that is not all that secure.

Can you identify manipulation strategies in Dawn's story? It is common for people who seek a partner for a particular reason to become involved in a manipulative relationship. When we say reason, we mean those reasons outside of genuine attraction and affection for another person. Now this is not to imply that people who become involved with someone due to a genuine liking and affection cannot be manipulated by their partner. After all, if their relationship becomes unhealthy, then one or both partners may develop patterns of manipulation. However, for those who engage in a relationship for a specific reason, such as money or power of some sort, manipulation may be more likely to occur. This is because one has something to offer that the other desperately wants; and to become involved with a person for a specific reason does imply desperation. Desperation naturally lends itself to manipulation.

Chapter 5 Psychological manipulation

Emotional or hidden manipulation can be characterized as a distinct impact through mental abuse, with the goal to control or extract benefits at the victim's expense.

It is crucial to recognize the substantial social impact of mental abuse stemming from manipulation. With manipulation, one individual is utilized to support another. The controller intentionally does whatever he needs to in order to best serve his interests, and his interests only.

Remember that not every person who acts according to these behaviors is purposely trying to manipulate you. However, it is critical to perceive these practices in circumstances where your rights, interests, and security are in question.

Signs of Emotional Manipulation

Manipulators will try to bring you to their "home turf," or at least a place where they are comfortable. This will end up making it easier for them to control you.

A manipulative individual may demand that you engage with them at a particular place like an office, home or public setting. This gives them a sense of control since they most likely scoped out the area before asking you there. That way, they are familiar with their surroundings while you may not know anything about the place yet. Cunning, but a simple way for manipulators to gain access to control.

Manipulators will give you a chance to have the first say to build up your courage before they address your shortcomings. Numerous sales reps do this when they decide whether you will be the perfect candidate to purchase what they are about to offer you. By posing general and examining inquiries, they build up a benchmark about your reasoning and conduct, from which they can then assess your qualities and shortcomings. This sort of addressing with a concealed plan can likewise happen at the work environment or with personal connections.

Manipulators know how to twist the truth, and they will get away with it because they don't always believe that they are even lying. They find a way to twist the truth so much that they believe it to be 100% true.

This can take place in the forms of lying, reason making, double-dealing, censuring the injured individual for causing their own exploitation, distortion of reality, exposure or retention of crucial data, misrepresentation, modest representation of the truth, and only seeing the truth in his or her own story.

Manipulators will sometimes overwhelm you by presenting you with a large amount of knowledge, sometimes in a confusing way. They exploit you by feeding false claims, measurements and other information you may not care to think about or investigate yourself.

This can occur in deals and financial circumstances, in expert-level conversations, or social interactions. By assuming control over you, the manipulator creates the perfect opportunity to ensnare you. A few people utilize this system to have a feeling of scholarly predominance.

Manipulators will often find ways to overpower you with formality. This means that they will blame their actions on rules or regulations, and things that are seemingly out of their control. Certain individuals use administration—desk work, techniques, laws, advisory groups, and different forms of red tape to advance their strategy of trying to get you to fall for their plan of manipulation.

This method can likewise be utilized to postpone the discovery of reality, conceal imperfections and shortcomings, and sidestep examination. Your boss might make you work on a holiday and explain that there was nothing he can do, even though he himself could have taken that same shift. This method is like him saying "I would if I could," even though the manipulator certainly has it in his power to change the situation.

Sometimes, a manipulator will raise their voice and show negative feelings. This can be a means of forceful control. When they complain loudly enough or show negative feelings that seem out of proportion for a situation, most reasonable people will submit to their intimidation and give them what they need to keep the peace, if for no better reason. The forceful voice is habitually joined with solid non-verbal communication, for example, standing or energized motions to heighten conflict.

Surprise is another common tactic manipulator might choose to use. They might use an outrageous statement, such as "you will never believe what the other person did to me," when telling a story. They also use unbelievable assertions, such as, "I was the only one doing any work today." These paint a surprising situation that can catch the other person off-guard, more likely to fall for the heightened truths the manipulator is sharing.

Regularly, the sudden negative information comes unexpectedly, so you have only a brief period to plan and counter. The controller may request extra concessions from you to keep working with you.

A manipulator might also not even give you the opportunity to choose in some situations. This is a typical deal and arrangement strategy, where the controller leans on you to settle on a choice before you are prepared.

A manipulator will have high expectations of you and demand high requests, ignoring that you might not be able to do what they are asking. They will make it seem like it's not even an option to say "no," even though what they are asking of you might be unreasonable in the first place.

By applying pressure and control, manipulators expect that you will split and yield to the manipulator's demands. Instead of saying, "Do you think you can do this?" they will simply ask, "When can you have this done?" never giving you the opportunity to agree to do something in the first place. This makes it hard for you to be able to say "no" to whatever it is that they might be requesting.

Manipulators will enjoy negative cleverness intended to jab at your shortcomings and weaken you. They will make sarcastic jokes to belittle you, and when you show hurt from these words, they will say, "I was just kidding," or "No big deal."

Manipulators like to make simple comments, frequently shrouded in wittiness or collegiality, to portray victims as second rate or deficient. These remarks can relate to appearance, traits, experience and qualifications, and the way that you strolled in two minutes late and exhausted.

By making you look terrible, and getting you to feel awful, the assailant wants to establish dominance over you. They also do this in an attempt to point things out about you that might change how others perceive you. While you might enjoy a certain musician that others think nothing of, a manipulator might say something like, "How could anyone like that band?"

The silent treatment is a popular tool used by manipulators. They know that ignoring you can sometimes be the best way to get under your skin. By intentionally not reacting to your calls, messages or requests, the manipulator presumes control by making you pause, and means to put uncertainty and vulnerability in your mind. Silence can sometimes be the most powerful of weapons.

They might not give you the silent treatment in person, but they can pretend to ignore you so that you aren't aware of their intentions. By pretending she doesn't understand what you need or what you need her to do, the manipulator makes you take on what is her duty and makes you sweat with effort and anxiety.

Kids utilize this strategy to defer tasks, delay demands upon them, and manipulate grown-ups into accomplishing for them what the kid would prefer not to do. Some adults use this strategy too, when they have a task they want to ignore, or a commitment they wish to evade. For example, intentionally mopping the floor poorly can trick the person in charge so that they decide not to delegate that task to you again.

On a larger scale, this can mean someone in a relationship pretends that they are unaware of what you might need on an emotional level. They'll say things like, "I don't understand what you want," even though they very well know what you need and simply aren't willing to put in the work to accomplish this goal.

This leads into how manipulators will often guilt trip you. Some examples may include blaming others instead of him or herself, focusing on their own weakness, acting as though someone else holds the key to their joy and achievement, or despondency and disappointment. By focusing guilt tripping others, the controller pressures the recipient into surrender.

Manipulators will then make sure to play the victim no matter how incorrect it might be. Some examples of this type of behavior include overstated or imagined individual issues, misrepresented or fabricated medical problems, reliance, codependency, conscious fragility to inspire compassion and support as well as playing frail or weak.

The reason for manipulators playing the victim is frequently to misuse the victim's goodwill, feelings of remorse, feelings of obligation and commitment, or eagerness to defend and support, to extricate preposterous advantages and concessions.

The expression "gaslighting" is frequently used to refer to manipulation that gets individuals to address themselves, their existence, memories, or musings. Gaslighting is basically when someone is going to try to make you feel crazy so that they can get away with their manipulative behavior. A manipulative individual may bend what you state and make it all about them, capture the discussion, or make you have an inclination that you've accomplished something terrible when you've done nothing wrong.

When you are being gaslighted, you may feel a misguided feeling of blame that you have done something terrible, even when that is not the situation. Manipulators blame; they do not accept any liability in a situation.

When you let a manipulator know that they hurt your feelings, they are instead going to point out how you are crazy, remembering things wrong, or being too sensitive about the situation.

As soon as someone does you a favor, not for the sake of "just because" but with hidden motives, you can almost be sure you are being manipulated. One essential sort of manipulator can be named "Mr. Nice Guy." This individual may be useful and complete a lot of favors for other individuals. Yet, with each great deed, there is a string attached—a desire. When you don't meet the manipulator's desire or motive, you will be described as unreasonable.

A sales rep, for instance, may influence your decision on purchasing a clothing item even though they don't think the item suits you. In a relationship, an accomplice may get you flowers right before asking you for a favor. These strategies work since they misuse social standards. It is typical to respond to favors, yet when somebody provides one deceitfully, we still feel constrained to acknowledge and go along.

Another method of manipulation is to inspire fear into someone, only to give them some relief afterwards. A person might scare you into going somewhere new, building your fear around the place. Then, they will strive to protect you and make you feel safe, even though the fears that they warned you about in the first place weren't real.

This can be done when you might be making an important decision. The manipulator will at first tell you all the reasons that you should be scared. They will tell you about the negative things that are going on and will do whatever they have to in order to ensure that you are fearful. Afterwards, they will come up with a solution so that they can make sure you are dependent on them and look up to them as a "savior" type.

Many different companies might use this tactic in order to sell you their product. For example, someone might make an elbow cream and on their commercial, tell you about how if you don't use it, you run the risk of getting a certain disease. Then, you will start to make sure to buy their product because you are scared of this disease, even though you never heard of it, or even thought about it, before watching the commercial.

Bribery is an effective tool of manipulators in certain circumstances. They can do it in obvious ways, saying something about how they'll give you money or a certain reward if you are able to do this thing for them. If you refuse, then they will start to use other manipulative tactics until they get what they want, sometimes even removing the bribe in the process so you end up walking away with no benefits at all.

Mirroring the target is a way that manipulators will manipulate. They can start to act like the other person so that the one being manipulated feels a closer connection to them. They might talk about similar struggles and challenging life issues they went through that are similar to the person who is being manipulated. For example, someone talking about how they struggle with grief after losing a few friends might find that their manipulator makes up or exaggerates a different death in order to try and relate to this person. They will then find that it is easier to control the person when they are feeling empathetic.

Storytelling is a common manipulation tactic. Manipulators will be experts at twisting a story to make sure that it suits their ends. They won't always completely make up new and original lies, but they will certainly twist the truth so that it sounds better for them, making them look like a hero, or the victim, whichever suits their needs at the given time that they are sharing the story.

Manipulators will learn how to set the mood of their victims. Though they are rigid in getting what they want, they can be very adaptable if it means having more control over a certain individual. If they know that someone likes a certain restaurant, they will take them there, or if they prefer to be alone and quiet at home, then they will do that.

It is not bad to take people to places they like, but if you are doing so to psychologically trick them into giving you something that you want, then that is when it turns into manipulation.

Controlling your voice is important for manipulators, as well as the gestures and touch that they use. They can be great actors, able to switch their voice and gestures at the drop of a hat. We all have different moods that might cause us to act different depending on the situation, but a true manipulator will wear many faces that they can switch whenever they want.

Manipulators often know the power of silence. Even though they might have endless tricks and conversations they can use on other people, at the end of the day, they will still know that being silent can sometimes be the most powerful thing that they do.

Less Common Manipulation Tactics

Maintaining an intent gaze can make individuals feel like they are being genuinely listened to. Manipulative individuals will make excellent eye contact and even take it a step further and enhance their eye contact with an engaged and invested facial expression.

A mesmerizing look is regularly given to test limits. Manipulators may do or say something awkward just previously or after the mesmerizing look to examine how you react. The look might feel like love or enticement. If somebody's mesmerizing look makes you feel off in any capacity, it is best to get up and take a break from the situation you find yourself in. Check your sentiments and remind yourself of your character and values if things get excessive.

Manipulators don't care about other people's body language and will instead overstep boundaries without much notice. Individuals who, in general, overstep boundaries have a specific appeal about them. Manipulative individuals will endeavor to break the rules in humble and at times playful ways. For example, they may step in front of you on the sidewalk just to check whether you'll permit it. Manipulative individuals might lift you off the ground amid embraces, and they'll find ways to attack your personal space.

Narcissists and manipulative individuals, generally speaking, stand nearer to others than other people do. They use space intrusion to threaten, show control, test limits, and to tempt. Manipulative individuals love using this tactic to promote power over you and entice you to give in to their needs or demands.

Sometimes a manipulator might share secrets with you without hesitation. They will do this as a tactic to keep you interested in them and to make them seem more approachable, relatable, and trustworthy. They might also do this because they are wanting you to reciprocate, sharing secrets that they can use against you. Then, when you confront the manipulator about the betrayal in the future, the manipulator will completely deny having ever said anything, making you feel crazy and defeated.

Manipulative individuals know how to sweet talk their victims. They also know how to keep you interested in what they are saying at all times. Manipulative individuals, as well as narcissists, are spinners of stories. When they get started about anything, it tends to be difficult to stop them.

Manipulative personalities will make you feel special by how frequently they trust in you. When they quit disclosing things to you, you may feel like you did something wrong and will do your best to get once more into their great graces. Creating this type of insecurity is tied in with controlling your time and focus, to secure your attention at the manipulator's whim. If you see someone manipulating you by selectively sharing and withholding, take a stride back and put some space between yourself and that individual.

Sometimes manipulators make use of pet names rather than your actual name. It might appear to be sweet when somebody begins calling you by a pet name. Be that as it may, manipulative identities will utilize words like "baby" or "dear" to belittle you. Then when they quit calling you by a pet name, it can create feelings of abandonment and leave you wondering what you fouled up. It is merely one more piece of their strategic maneuvers. If such names bother you, reveal to them that you don't value being called pet names and would instead like to be called by your real name.

When somebody compliments you a great deal, obviously you are going to feel good about yourself. It is essential to distinguish what their actual intentions are. Some of the time, individuals will utilize compliments to get something out of you.

If you possess authority at your job, school, or other professional setting, individuals with less authority or at a lower position than you may utilize compliments with expectations of an advancement. If the individual complimenting you is at an equal level, it could be a legitimate compliment with no manipulative thought processes. Of course, male-female relationships complicate these matters further. Even in a scenario between equals in the work setting, a compliment could be used as manipulation to advance a social agenda.

Not everyone who gives compliments means to manipulate you. It's wise to be aware of individuals' actual expectations. Trust your instinct. If something feels off about somebody, it may be beneficial to find why.

Keeping yourself from falling for manipulative strategies may take some training. A conventional method to tell if you are in a relationship, or simply having a conversation with an individual who's attempting to manipulate you, is to focus on where they bring the conversation. If they are endeavoring to make you feel either exceptionally fortunate or unfortunate about yourself, that's an important warning sign.

It is essential, however, to note that the above explanations do not guarantee you are dealing with a manipulative person. Using pet names, for example, does not mean you or an associate is manipulative. To analyze manipulators, you need to take their entire character into account and not only specific attributes of their behavior.

Chapter 6 Primary types of analysis

Now that you are clear on why analysis is used and why it is so essential to your manipulation practice, it is time for you to learn how you can actually analyze people! In this chapter, you are going to learn about three primary types of analysis, as well as when you can use them and how you can maintain your secrecy in the process. The three main strategies we are going to pay attention to are: body language (including facial expressions), profiling, and verbal cues. These three areas are the most important when it comes to analyzing someone prior to manipulation.

Body Language

There are two types of body language that you want to pay attention to when you are reading someone's physical expressions: their actual body language, and their facial expressions. Both of these will give you a large amount of insight as to what they are thinking and how they are feeling at any given time.

You want to begin by paying attention to someone's body language before you even begin talking to them. Get a sense of how they carry themselves, how they tend to move and express themselves when different types of things are said to them, and how their body language changes when different moods are experienced. Ideally, the longer you can comfortably observe someone from a distance, the better. This gives you a chance to get a stronger idea of who they are and what they are like before you enter a conversation with them. However, there are many times that you do not get a significantly long period of time to analyze someone before you begin your conversation. In these circumstances, it is beneficial to have already spent time practicing analyzing people and then use this practice to generate an idea of how your target is feeling and their personality in a short amount of time.

When you are reading someone's body language, start by getting a "baseline" of what they are normally like. Pay attention to their face, their arms and hands, and their feet. Also, if they are walking, notice their gait and how quickly or slowly they are walking. You also want to know how they are carrying themselves. Then, once you get a baseline, take a moment to pay attention to how their baseline changes with different stimulus. For example, when they are happy or when they are annoyed. You want to essentially get an idea of their three primary states that matter most to you: normal, positive, and negative. This will help you when it comes to conversing, as it will give you an idea of whether they are having a positive or negative reaction to what you are saying to them.

The benefit of body language is that virtually everyone has a similar type of body language expression. This is a form of communication that we unknowingly learn as we grow up, and because we all tend to communicate in the same way, our body language tends to work in the same way from person to person. For this reason, if you do not have a long time to observe or analyze someone first, you can use basic body language knowledge to generate an idea of what they are thinking and feeling, and about how they are feeling in response to various things you say or offer them. Now that you understand body language and how you should be reading it, let's start focusing on specific cues and readings that you can understand from someone when you are analyzing them. In the following sections we are going to explore three types of body language: the body language itself, walking or mobile body language, and facial expressions.

Forms of Body Language

Body language comes in two forms: basic cues, and complex cues. Basic cues are ones that you are likely already familiar with. They include ones such as stomping your feet or making fists with your hands when you are angry, slouching in your chair and resting your head in your hands when you are bored or upset about something, and other similar cues. You are likely already familiar with the majority of basic body language cues, so we are going to focus more on the in-depth cues here. Complex body language are things we unconsciously do any time we are feeling a certain way. These cues give on-lookers the ability to know exactly how we are feeling. Most people looking at us only know subconsciously and get a "feeling" about how we are feeling, or they may even overlook it entirely in favor of their own thoughts and feelings. As an experienced body language reader, however, you would be able to easily identify what these cues mean and how they relate to what the person is thinking at any given time. Let's take a look at them, now. When you are reading body language, you typically want to start with getting an idea for a person's overall body language. This is how they tend to carry themselves when they are "at rest" in the conversation. It may vary from conversation to conversation depending on their pre-existing emotions at any given time, but in general you should notice that most people have a fairly neutral "starting" position. Knowing what someone tends to look like when they are in neutral allows you to recognize when they make changes and what these changes mean about how they are feeling and what they are thinking.

To read someone's complex body language, start by looking at their hands and arms. Where are they placed, and what are they doing? Are they near the body, or further away? In general, the further the hands are from the body, the more relaxed a person is feeling. This is true unless the hands are tucked in neatly but are completely relaxed and not tensing, fidgeting, or grasping at anything. If their hand is rested comfortably on their lap, for example, it would show that the person somewhat submissive and relaxed. If both of their hands were folded and rested in the center of their lap, it would show that they were completely submissive in the situation. When people touch their arms with opposing hands, this often signifies that they are feeling uncomfortable or uncertain in a situation and that they are trying to understand it at a greater level. If both hands are touching the opposing arms, however, this indicates that they are feeling shut down on some level. If the hands are relaxed on the opposing arms, the person is feeling defeated. If they are tense, the person is feeling agitated. Sometimes, hands may not be positioned on the body itself at all. Instead, they may be placed elsewhere. For example, on an object. The message then comes from whatever that object is and the tension of the grip on that object. For example, if they are lightly gripping their cup in front of them, they are relaxed but waiting for an appropriate moment to take a drink. If they are holding their purse or keys in their hand, they are ready to leave but are waiting for the right time to say that they are ready to go. If their hands never left their purse or keys, it means they were not intending to stay long and that they may be uncomfortable or untrusting in their surroundings. With hands, there are two things you are looking for: placement, and grip. If the hands are placed on an object, consider what that object means to them. If the object is something that the person would typically use if they stay around for a while, then the person is likely relaxed and well-engaged in their environment. If they are gripping anything such as their keys, their purse, their wallet, the door handle, or otherwise, this means that they are ready to go and do not want to be here any longer. The next place you want to look is at their legs and their feet. Unlike the hands, feet do not grip anything. For that reason, the biggest thing you can learn about someone from their feet comes from which direction the feet are pointing and what movements they are making, if any. Where the feet are pointing says a great deal about what the person is thinking and where they want to go. If, for example, they are pointed at the person in front of them and at the door, that means that they want to leave with that person. If both are pointed at the person, they are comfortable in the environment and completely tuned in to that single person. If they are pointing at multiple people in the conversation, they are engaged in a group conversation. If they are pointing at the bar, they want another drink. If both are pointing at the door, they really want to leave.

The feet may be making a variety of different movements, too. If they are still, this means that the person is either relaxed or focused. They are engaged in whatever is going on around them, and so they are not thinking about any movements. When they begin to move, however, they can signify a variety of things. For example, if a person is feeling anxious, they may rapidly move their feet back and forth. If the feet are only gently rocking back and forth, or if you are looking at a woman and she is slipping the back of her shoe on and off, it means that they are feeling some form of attraction for the person that they are talking to. If a person has their feet crossed at the ankles and they are bouncing them around, this may signify that they are bored and wish that they were somewhere else, or doing something else.

Pay attention to both the hands and the feet when you are reading someone's body language. Both will give you a clear identifying factor of how they are feeling and what they are thinking. The best way to get a full read on a person is to read what both parts of the body are telling you and then put it together as a full message. That way, you know exactly what the person is thinking and feeling.

Walking Cues

How people walk says a lot about how they are feeling in any given moment. In general, the faster they are walking, the less they are thinking. This doesn't necessarily mean that they aren't thinking about anything it all. Instead, it usually means that they are only thinking about one thing. For example, they may be late and they are thinking about what they are late for and so they are walking fast. Or, they may be angry and looking for the person they are upset with, and the only thing on their mind is that anger. Since the faster a person walks translates to less thoughts on a person's mind, the slower a person walks translates to more thoughts on a person's mind. Therefore, if you see someone walking about slowly, they are often thinking about a lot. They may be walking slowly with an inquisitive look on their face, as though they are pondering something large and looking for the answer while they walk. Or, they may be walking slowly with a somewhat dazed look on their face, thinking about anything that comes to their mind.

Aside from the speed of a person's walk, think about their posture, too. A person who walks with a tall, straight back and their head held high is one who is confident and sure of themselves. Someone who walks with their shoulders slumped down and their back shrugged forward and barely picks up their feet is someone who is feeling unconfident. If a person generally walks with a tall, straight posture, and you see them walking with a shrunken, slumped posture, this likely means that they are upset about something in the moment. If the opposite happens, then the person is likely happy and has experienced some form of achievement in the very recent past. In general, the taller and straighter someone's posture is when they are walking, the surer of themselves they are. This can go all the way up to them having their chin turned upwards as they look down their nose at people, meaning that they likely have a grandiose sense of self-worth. Likewise, the more shrunken and slumped their posture is, the less sure they are of themselves. This goes all the way down to being completely slumped and skulking along, showing that they are feeling really low and down on their luck.

Facial Expressions

There are three areas you want to pay attention to one someone's face when you are using it as a tool for analysis. These three areas include the mouth, cheeks, and eyebrows. These three parts of the face have the tendency to move the most when it comes to expressive looks, and therefore they will also tell you the most about what a person is thinking or feeling at any given time. Facial expressions change rapidly throughout conversations, so pay close attention to these. In general, an emotion will first be expressed on the face, then into the body. They say that if a negative emotion is already being expressed in the body, it's too late and you may have lost the trust and faith of your target when it comes to manipulation. You have to be very swift and confident to turn that emotion around and regain their attention and trust.

With the mouth, there are many things you can tell. For example, someone who's mouth is soft and relaxed is either bored or uninterested in what you are presently talking about. You are losing their attention, and fast. If their mouth is slightly pursed, this is usually the sign that the person is interested in what you are saying and that you have their focus. If the mouth is tightly pursed or even pushed out slightly, this would indicate that they are angry and trying to "bite their tongue" from what they want to say. Smiling typically indicates happiness, but smiling with soft eyes that do not feature crow's feet at the sides indicates that the smile may be out of nervousness or obligation. A true smile always results in the eyes crunching and expressing crow's feet at the sides. If someone's mouth is pulled down at the sides, it may indicate they are sad. However, if it is pulled down and tense in any way, it may instead indicate defensiveness or annoyance. The biggest thing to pay attention for in someone's cheeks is their tension. If someone's cheeks are tight and pulled back towards the ears, this typically indicates that the person is feeling fearful or nervous. If they are tight and pushed forward toward the mouth, this would mean that the person is feeling angry. If the person's cheeks are tight and pressed up toward the eyes, this would indicate that the person is feeling happy. If they are soft or seem to be drooping toward the floor, this would indicate that the person is feeling sad.

Lastly, the eyebrows are another expressive place on the face that you need to pay attention to. If a person's eyebrows are pulled down at the edges and turned upward slightly in the center, this would indicate that they are feeling sad or even pitiful. If they are furrowed, this would mean that they are focusing and trying to take everything in. However, if they furrow and their entire face tenses up, this would indicate that they are angry. Eyebrows that stay lightly raised for the entire conversation indicate that the person is interested in what you are talking about. However, eyebrows that quickly flicker up and then down indicate that a person is surprised by a piece of information. If they are fairly neutral and don't move, this means the person may be disinterested.

Profiling

Profiling is where you look at someone's surroundings to get a better idea of who they are. This can be easy in some cases, and harder in others. Let's take a look at the three main areas you want to pay attention to with profiling: who they are with, what they look like, and their environment.

Who Are They With?

Start with who the person is with. If the person is close with the person or people they have come in with, then the interactions you see between those two people will be more accurate to how that person feels when they are comfortable. It also allows you to look at the pair or group as a whole to get a feel for what they are like. For example, if they are all dressed in a country-esque theme, you can conclude that they may be more outdoorsy and do-it-yourself type people. However, if they are all dressed in business or business casual clothes, their preferences may lean more toward outsourcing things and getting the best of the best - already made for them. If they are with people they are not typically with, you will be able to tell as the interactions will be a little tenser between them. Although they may still be comfortable, especially if the person is confident, it may seem a little more professional than casual, even if they aren't together for anything business-related.

What Do They Look Like?

Pay attention specifically to what the person you are targeting looks like. Are they well-groomed? Do they look after themselves well? Or are they unkempt and looking somewhat messy? This can give you an idea of how they feel about themselves, and how they think others feel about them, too. If they are well-dressed and groomed, this would indicate that they are confident and care what other people think and want to be perceived well by others. If they are unkempt and not well groomed, it may indicate that they feel low on self-esteem and self-confidence and that they don't overly care about what other people think of them because they don't think that they are worth high praise in the first place. In addition, pay attention to what they are wearing. Their sense of style will tell you a lot about who they are. Bold, bright clothes that have fancy designs, for example, indicate that a person's personality would be bold, bright, and unique. If their clothes are boxy, unfitted, and dull, however, the person may lack individuality and not have a clear sense of who they are. Someone who dresses neatly and in neutral colors likely believes everything should be clean-cut and modern, and has a fairly similar clean-cut personality to match it.

What Is Their Environment?

Lastly, pay attention to their environment. The places they spend the most of their time equate to the places they feel most comfortable in. If they're spending a lot of time at concerts and at friend's houses, this would clearly indicate that they are outgoing and into a party lifestyle. If they are regularly spending time at up-scale bars, high end fashion boutiques and galas, this would indicate that they are a part of "high society" and that they like things to be the best of the best. If you can, pay attention to their home, or how they keep their work space and car, too. If they keep them clean and organized, this indicates that the person is someone who has a clear frame of mind and works best in a clear and organized space. If they keep things messy and chaotic, it likely reflects on a disorganized frame of mind and an uncertainty about things. They are also less likely to be reliable than those who are more clean and organized.

Chapter 7 The Most Powerful Mind-Power Tool

Humans spend countless hours seeking new ways to work just about anything. Through endless hours of research, they pour over books and journals looking for the message that will tell them the secret to harnessing mind power. Many never realize that the most powerful mind power tool is already on board and just aching to be used. It is the human brain, the mind itself.

Every time a person practices a new habit or thinks a new thought, they make a new pathway in the brain. Every time the habit is used, or the idea is thought, the nerve pathway becomes even stronger. The human brain is wired at birth to be an efficient machine and it is ready, from birth, to make an ever-increasing amount of nerve pathways and to strengthen the pathways that are used the most.

Sometimes thoughts and habits need to be changed for the improvement of the person. When people decide that they would like to make a change in their lives, there will be a period of adjustment. This is true whether the change is mental, emotional, or physical. During this period of adjustment, there will be some level of discomfort. When a habit or a thought is already formed, it has made its own path in the brain. When a stimulus is seen or heard, the message travels along the preset nerve pathway to the spot in the brain that controls that thought or habit. In order to change a thought or a habit, it is necessary for the nerve path to be changed. Until the nerve path is changed, the old nerve path will remain in the brain. The discomfort comes from the brain trying to automatically access the old pathway and the new pathway at the same time. This is painful for the brain to do.

It is easy to become frustrated when the brain goes back to its old patterns of thought and habit. Never fall into the habit of placing blame on a lack of willpower. Willpower has nothing to do with it. It is a very difficult thing to override preset pathways in the brain. The brain is a very powerful tool. When will power fails and mistakes happen, remember to use kindness and compassion in dealing with the failure. The brain is very efficient at doing what it does. The only way to change the pathways in the brain is to keep working on new pathways that will eventually obliterate the old, undesirable ones.

The brain needs a clear understanding that changes are about to take place and new pathways are about to be laid down. Remind the brain that new habits and new thoughts will be replacing the old ones. Blaming failure on a lack of will power is a self-defeating statement. The process of making new nerve paths in the brain takes hard work and time. It will help to keep reminding oneself of the impending change. By doing this over and over, it makes the process no longer about possible character flaws. The focus is now put on the habit of thought that is being built.

Is it possible to build new nerve pathways in the brain? Yes, it is possible, and it can be done. If more proof is needed, just compare the adult brain to the baby's brain. Every current habit and thought a person has is the direct result of having spent time practicing them over and over until they created a pathway in the brain. New pathways can be created. Think of it this way: they already have. The baby's brain has no idea of anything. It has no thoughts or habits. Every nerve path currently in the brain was practiced until it became a part of the brain. Think of the baby. The baby lies around day after day and does baby things. Then one day the baby notices the shiny rattle that mommy is waving in front of its little face. The baby wants the rattle. As the baby is waving its tiny arms around, the mommy puts the rattle close enough so the baby can touch it with its wavering hand. After a few of these sessions, the baby gets the idea that if the arm is in the air it can touch the rattle. A nerve pathway is beginning to grow. So the baby decides to lift its arm to actively reach for the rattle. The baby will be unsuccessful at first because the arms will wave wildly and will not connect with the rattle. One day, the baby will actually grab the rattle, and the nerve pathway is then complete.

While this may seem like a very simple example, it is exactly how nerve pathways are created in the brain. Every action, thought, or habit has its own nerve pathway. All pathways must be created. No one was born knowing to sit in front of the television and mindlessly eat dip with chips. No one was born lamenting the excess pounds they carry in strange places. No one was born hating their body. All behaviors are learned, good and bad. And the bad ones can be replaced with good ones.

So if the ability to program negative thoughts into the brain exists, then the ability to disrupt those negative thoughts with positive thoughts also exists. The brain can be reprogrammed. It is a powerful tool, and its main function is to turn thoughts into reality. The brain is always working, so why not use the power of the brain to benefit rather than harm? Just because a particular habit or thought has been around all forever does not mean it needs to stay. Use the power of the brain to choose new habits and thoughts to focus on and replace the old, negative thought pathways in the brain.

The new thought needs to be believable; the new habit needs to be doable. It does not real good to try to stick to a habit that is impossible to accomplish or to try to believe a thought that is unbelievable. After years of seeing the reality of an obese body, it would be nearly impossible to suddenly believe that the image in the mirror is that of a skinny person. But the brain will likely accept something that mentions learning to take care of the body or learning to accept the body in order to correct its flaws. The brain will turn a belief in reality. Believing a positive thought will lead to quite a different result than the ending where only negative thoughts are present.

Be prepared to repeat and repeat some more. The primary key to being able to make a new habit stay is repeating it constantly. The more a new, desirable habit is practiced, the more the brain begins to accept it. The nerve path becomes stronger every day. With constant practice, this new nerve path will become the path the brain will prefer to use, and the old one will cease to exist.

In any case, be sure to allow enough time to effectively create a change. Accept the starting point and constantly visualize the ending point. Accept the fact that the path to the goal of a new habit or thought will not be easy or perfect. The path will almost never travel in a straight line. Sometimes people fall completely off the path, and that is okay too. Just get back up and get back on. Do not get sidetracked by the idea that this journey will be easy and carefree because it will not be. Just keep thinking of the new nerve pathway that will be created by the new thought or habit and it will eventually become a reality.

Most of the pathways in the brain are stored in the subconscious mind. This is the part of the mind that is always working without always being thought of. Think of learned skills like tying shoes, zipping a coat, and pouring milk into a glass. These were all learned behavior whose nerve pathways are firmly set in the subconscious part of the mind. This part of the brain is the bank of data for all life functions.

The communication between the conscious mind and the unconscious mind works in both directions. Whenever a person has a memory, and emotion, or an idea, it is rooted in the subconscious mind and translated to the conscious mind through mind power. The subconscious has the power to control just about anything a human does regularly.

For example, during meditation steady, deep breathing is usually practiced. The control of the breath is brought from the subconscious mind and given to the conscious mind to tell it to control the breathing. Once a pattern of deep steady breathing is begun by the conscious mind, the subconscious mind takes over and keeps the set rhythm going until it is told to stop. This is done by a conscious end to the deep breathing or an encounter with an outside stimulus like stress. The subconscious mind also processes the great wealth of information received daily and only passes along to the conscious mind those things that are necessary for the brain to remember.

When sending thoughts from the conscious mind to the subconscious mind, the brain will only send those thoughts that are attached to great emotion. The only thoughts that remain in the subconscious are those that are kept there with strong emotions. Unfortunately, the brain does not know the difference between positive emotions and negative emotions. Any strong emotion will work. Both negative emotions and positive emotions can be quite strong. Also, unfortunately, negative emotions tend to be stronger than positive emotions.

Step one in learning to use the power of the subconscious part of the mind will be to eliminate any thoughts that come with negative emotions. Also, negative mental comments will also need to cease. Fears will usually come true, specifically because they are drowning in negative emotion. This is why negative ideas need to be eliminated because they can be very harmful roadblocks on the road to harnessing brain power.

One best practice to use to get rid of negative thoughts is to counter them with positive thoughts. This will take time and practice, but it is a very powerful and useful technique. Whenever a negative thought pops in the conscious mind, immediately counter it with a positive thought that is dripping with strong emotion. The actual truth will come out somewhere in between the two thoughts.

Another way to counter negative emotions is to delete them, just like using a remote control. When a negative thought comes into the conscious mind, imagine destroying it. Imagine writing that thought on paper and burning it. Imagine pointing a remote control at the thought and pressing a huge delete button. Whatever form used to imagine deleting the thought, the important thing is to get rid of it before it can take hold in the subconscious mind.

Find something energizing and use it to reach a goal. Those things that are found to be energizing bring boundless energy to positive thoughts. It is often necessary to invent motivation, at least in the beginning, to learn to create new habits and thoughts. But with a bit of practice and a lot of positive thought, new positive habits will soon be burned into the subconscious mind and the old negative thoughts and habit will fade away.

How Does It Make The Victim Feel?

There are likely to be many thoughts and feelings going around a victim's head but confused is probably the main one.

Most people who have been a victim to mental manipulation know deep down that something isn't quite right, perhaps a nagging voice or intuitive thought that it screaming 'don't listen', but it's on mute or isn't quite loud enough. It could very well be that this person knows what they're dealing with, but they're not quite ready to go. They still hang onto the thought that this person has some good in them, perhaps that they can save them.

You cannot save or right the actions of a person who uses mental manipulation as a control tactic. The only thing you can do is walk away. Of course, that is far easier said than done.

We've mentioned before that a person who has undergone a period of manipulation of this kind is quite likely to be emotionally scarred and damaged once the ordeal is over. It may be that they never feel that they want to connect to another person again, they may develop severe trust issues, and they may also find it extremely difficult to be intimate with another person in the future.

It's important for a person who has been subject to abuse of this kind to seek professional help to allow them to unpick what has happened and really solidify in their mind the facts. Even years afterward it's not unusual for a person to not quite 100% believe what happened. They might still have some glimmer of thinking they were wrong, or that they might have imagined something. It's important to go through a professional route and really get to the heart of what happened. This is important for future relationships and future happiness because otherwise, the whole cycle is likely to repeat itself.

Many victims of manipulation also develop anxiety, depression, or even PTSD (post-traumatic stress disorder), depending on how severe the experience was.

Whilst the ordeal is actually happening, aside from confusion, the constant questioning of their own sanity can cause a person to shrink into themselves. In this case, they might stop going out, stop seeing friends, and therefore cut themselves off from those who are open to helping them. They may become depressed, lose interest in their work, and have no hope for the future. This is exactly the outcome that a manipulator wants because when this happens, they really do have the victim under their thumb, and he or she is not going anywhere.

Put simply, mental manipulation can, in some cases, destroy a person.

What's Really Going On Under The Surface

So, underneath all of this, what is really happening? Is this person evil? Do they want to watch someone they claim to care about whither away to nothing?

Nobody can tell, but in most cases, it's not really that sinister. We mentioned narcissists before, and a person with true NPD doesn't actually want to ruin or destroy another person, they simply cannot understand why they can't see things from their side. They are literally at a loss to understand why this person is not understanding their level of self-importance.

There are many different types of narcissists, ranging from mild to moderate, and some a little more severe, but there is one particular type which basically cannot be saved without extreme therapy. This is the malignant narcissist.

A malignant narcissist is a sociopath, some might even say psychopath in some cases, and they will twist, turn, manipulate, deceive, and ruin another person for their own gains. The terrifying thing about this type of narcissist is that most will never seek treatment because they are so deeply into themselves that they really can't see anything wrong. Whilst we're not suggesting all narcissists of this kind are going to go out and commit a terrible crime against another person, there have been instances in the past where serial killers or other criminals have been unearthed to have malignant narcissistic personalities.

How can you tell if you're in the midst of one? You probably won't until it's too late, and when you do realize what's going on, you need to get away as quickly as possible. In this case, you will probably need emotional support afterward, to understand what happened and to help you realize that none of it was your fault, that you really weren't going crazy.

At the midst of it all, that is what a victim is going to feel like - that they are going crazy, and that in itself is a terrible, out of control, feeling. The fact is that a manipulator feeds off of this vulnerability because they are so lacking in their own confidence and self-worth.

This chapter has covered a lot of ground in terms of the dynamics of what goes in a manipulative situation such as this, and what types of tactics may be used. Now, do not worry about this too much. Manipulative narcissists are quite rare, but it's important to highlight their existence when talking about the very subject that this type of person lives for.

Nobody can 100% tell you why a person would be mentally manipulative towards another. We can speculate and give examples of why it has happened in the past, but as of yet, we are unable to get into another person's head and really examine their thoughts! Perhaps when that type of technology comes we will learn more about this type of behavior but for now, it's best to focus on awareness. This means understanding what techniques are used, being able to spot them, and learning how to deal with the experience and kick it out of your life. Of course, in most situations, this also means walking away from the person who is causing you such mental anguish.

How Manipulators Use Neuro-Linguistic Programming to Change Your Thought Processes

The human brain works in confusing and complicated ways, with various pathways connecting our thoughts, emotions, and what we perceive reality to be. Of course, you can train your brain to think or feel anything if you focus on it for long enough, and at the heart of all psychological processes, including cognitive behavioral therapy (CBT) is that very type of brain training.

There is however a form of training which can be used for good but can also be misused for bad. This is called Neuro-linguistic programming, or NLP for short.

Whether or not a manipulator has inside knowledge of what they are doing psychologically or whether it is simply a tactic they feel works from the reactions of the person they're close to remains to be seen, but NLP is regularly used to manipulate a victim into questioning their reality, and therefore questioning their own sanity. Is gaslighting a form of NLP? In some ways, but we'll talk about that in a short while in a little more detail. NLP in itself is a quite subtle and complex process, but an extremely effective way to alter someone's thought processes, simply by using clever words and phrases.

Chapter 8 How To Improve Your People Reading Skills

One way of improving your people reading skills is to observe people in your daily life. Like any form of reading, one has to frequently engage in reading other people. The best starting point is the people close to you as you get to test the accuracy of your body language reading skills. For instance, observe your roommate's bodily cues and try to guess his or her emotional status.

Even though it might appear as spying on the person, you can go ahead and label the person as Specimen Y and maintain a journal of their non-verbal communication and what you concluded. When reading the body language of a person, the intention is not to judge them or correct them but to accurately determine how they are feeling without asking the individual verbally.

Focus more on people in groups as most try to mimic each other. Reading people in groups is important because in most cases, people are in social contexts where they are several people.

People in groups such as in a class, a stadium or workplace tend to mimic each other. If one person takes a selfie, chances are that the others will also take selfies. If one person starts taking a walk, chances are that the rest will also join inadvertently. It appears that when an individual is placed in a group setting, then he or she is likely to let others dictate how they act and react. In most cases, people will deliberately suppress undesired emotions and actions to accommodate others or simply fit in. Against this backdrop, reading people in a group can improve your effective body language reading competencies

Equally important, you should exhibit awareness. You should pay attention to everything that the person is doing and when the person is doing it. While this appears trivial, each small and subtle detail about the target person is necessary for one to accurately profile the person. For instance, if the target person adjusts earing, you should not assume that this is a mundane aspect and does not constitute body language. Being awake to every aspect of behavior, actions, and movements of the target person are critical to effectively reading the non-verbal cues of the individual. Awareness requires that you also understand yourself first, and this can be realized through emotional intelligence competencies.

For emphasis, study people you admire. Another way of attaining this is to find any recordings or videos of the people, mute the voice and study only the body language. With social media, people are sharing videos and audio recordings that one can learn from. You can also get a movie, especially the one that you are to watch, mute the volume, and analyze the non-verbal communication. Then get a paper and profile each of the characters observed on their personality and emotion. Once you have completed the profiling, activate the volume, and compare the perceived character against the cues that you have interpreted.

Another way is to read the body language is to connect with the person to determine the truthfulness of their emotions and personality. Try to mirror the target person by mimicking their body positions, matching their tone, and carrying the same pace of the conversation. When mimicking the individual, ensure that it is done in a subtle manner. Through mirroring, one creates a synergy and connection which enables you gets into the mind of the target person. Mimicking another person's bodily cues should be carefully done to avoid making it appear like you are trying to flirt or that you are creepy.

Look for additional cues when you encounter that the target person is crossing their arms and legs. Crossing the arms and legs denotes that one is defensive, but most people cross their arms and legs when feeling comfortable or if they want to concentrate more about what is being spoken.

If someone holds a drink on the table using the opposite hand, then the person is showing a lack of confidence. In overall, body language cues should be read as an entire set as focusing on one can be misleading. Where necessary, consider the cultural or learned behavior that may elicit a different meaning from what the non-verbal communication is suggesting. For instance, people that stammer may throw gestures randomly or stomp their feet, and this does not imply that they are lacking confidence or are scared.

Focus more on eye contact of the individual. You can initiate eye contact with the target person and observe their eye contact behavior. Eye contact, just like touch, communicates much more about the person and their emotional status. Staring at the ceiling or on the floor may indicate that the individual is bored and not interested in what is being said.

However, an individual may look on the floor or stare at the ceiling if the news being given is negative and painful such as the loss of a friend or loss of a job. In this context, avoiding eye contact does not imply that the individual is not listening, but instead, the person is thinking deeper about how to navigate the negative emotions. There are also extreme situations where eye contact can mislead, such as people that shy who will avoid eye contact.

Equally important is that you should watch for the shoulder posture of the target person to read their body language. If the person holds their shoulders by their ears, then it is a sign of tension and can make the speaker become unease as well. Relaxed shoulders indicate that one is feeling calm and alert. If the person tries to retract the shoulders closer to the trunk of the body as if an umbrella closing, then the person is feeling embarrassed or unease with the environment or the message being passed. Fortunately, the posture of the shoulders can be read from a distant position.

Another area that can help you improve body reading is the sitting posture of the individual. Slouching on the seat suggests casualness or tiredness of the target person. If the person spreads their legs wide while seated, then it indicates that the individual is not participating in the conversation.

Crossing the legs may indicate that the person is feeling unease or relaxed when participating in the conversation. It is important that you take note of the sitting posture of the target person as it communicates about the attitude and emotional status of the individual. It might be necessary to walk near the audience and take note of their sitting posture.

Like any form of reading, recognize and address personal bias and stereotypes. Each one of us has ingrained biases and stereotypes, which is largely a function of our parenting and environment. For instance, if you grew up in a strict Christian family, then you may show disdain to an atheist, and the contrary is true. There are visible attributes of a person that can trigger biases that will distract making an objective conclusion about the target individual.

For instance, the skin color or gender of the target person can distort the objective reading of the target individual. If you are a man and you notice that the target person, a woman is staring at the neighbor who is a man also then your biases may make you think they are in love because that is how you view women. It is important to recognize and work on personal biases to help you objectively profile the target person.

If there is an opportunity, study, and analyze the handshake or hug offered by the target person. When analyzing the handshake, try to assess it in combination with the facial expression exhibited. For instance, if you shake the hand of the other person and the person shakes your hand firmly but looks down then the person could be naturally shy, and this may imply that the person is confident as the one that shakes the hand firmly and maintains eye contact.

On the other hand, if you shake the hand of the person and the individual firmly shakes your hand but frowns, then the person could be feeling unease and irked by your previous behavior or comments.

Lastly, like any other form of reading competencies, it is necessary to prepare for reading people by going through resources that discuss and analyze communicative cues. For instance, get a book or presentation or documentaries on body language and study them. You can only analyze what you know at first. For instance, there several aspects of touch that people do not and will not take them into consideration when reading touch.

The same is true for posture and facial expressions. The more theoretical knowledge you have on body language, the more effective you will be at reading the non-verbal cues of people.

Activity

Search for TV series "Gary Unmarried" and pick one episode then focus on the character Dr. Walter Krandall who was Gary and Allison marriage counselor. Assess how effective he is in reading the body language of Gary and Allison.

Conclusion

I hope you have learned valuable information that will help you stay vigilant and protect yourself against the machinations of the manipulative and controlling people that you encounter in all walks of life.

The next step is to start reviewing all of your relationships and figuring out whether they are tainted by any of the manipulation techniques that we have talked about in this book. To have relationships that are truly healthy and beneficial to you, it's important to make sure that they are not based on manipulation.

You might have settled into certain habits or patterns with your partner, family members, friends, and colleagues, without even realizing that you were emotionally exploited. As you review those dynamics, identify any areas where you feel emotionally shortchanged, and use what you have learned here to rectify the situations.

From this point on, you have to learn to stand up for yourself in order to defeat the manipulative agendas of others. Don't let anyone manipulate you by victimizing you, playing with your emotions, lying to you, using your weaknesses against you, or even by smothering you with affection.

Even though we have looked at the dark aspects of human nature in this book, it's important for you to remember that people are generally good, so don't close yourself off to new experiences out of fear of being manipulated. You can have happy and healthy relationships with people if you encourage them to join you on your journey to emotional maturity.

If this book has been useful to you and you like it, I suggest you also read these my books

"How to analyze people"

"Body language of people"

"Persuasion Skills"

www.ingramcontent.com/pod-product-compliance
Lightning Source LLC
Chambersburg PA
CBHW070713250726

48662CB00001B/394